PALEO
SLOW COOKING

Publications International, Ltd.

Photography on pages 5, 6 and 12 by Shutterstock Images.

Crock-Pot® and the Crock-Pot® logo are registered trademarks of Sunbeam Products, Inc. used under license.

Recipe Development: Recipes on pages 18, 22, 24, 26, 44, 64, 82, 108, 114, 116, 122, 140, 142 and 162 by David Bonom.

Pictured on the front cover: Cajun Pot Roast *(page 40)*.
Pictured on the back cover *(clockwise from top left):* Spicy Citrus Pork with Pineapple Salsa *(page 66),* Braised Lamb Shanks *(page 18)*, Curried Chicken and Coconut Soup *(page 96)* and Pulled Pork with Honey-Chipotle Barbecue Sauce *(page 64)*.

ISBN: 978-1-68022-088-9

Library of Congress Control Number: 2015943910

Manufactured in China.

8 7 6 5 4 3 2 1

TABLE OF CONTENTS

THE PALEO PRINCIPLES

A NEW DIET THAT'S 100,000 YEARS OLD: PALEO

Humans were hunter-gatherers for tens of thousands of years. They ate the wild plants they could find and the meat they could kill. Why should we care what they ate? One reason is that after all these centuries, our DNA is still virtually identical to theirs.

The most profound and recent change in the way humans live and eat resulted from the invention of agriculture, which began less than 10,000 years ago—a mere drop in the bucket in evolutionary history. Agriculture allowed us to go from a diet of lean meat and lots of different kinds of fruits and vegetables to one based primarily on grains and starchy crops.

There is quite a lot of anthropological evidence that this change was not healthy for Homo sapiens. Studies of early agricultural societies indicate that they had shorter life spans, more malnutrition and were shorter in stature than their Paleolithic forebears. Agriculture allowed us to stay in one place, to feed more people and to develop culture. Nobody wants to go back to the Stone Age. But since our genetic make-up hasn't changed, maybe, just maybe, the modern high-carb, low-fat diet isn't the ideal for us.

BUT I'M NOT A CAVEMAN!

Our lives are (thank heavens!) very different, but our digestive systems may not be. Obviously we can't literally eat what Paleo man did. Nobody wants to dine on bison brain with a side of bitter greens. What the Paleo diet proposes is that we learn from what worked and find modern healthy equivalents. It's not complicated. It's an invitation to change your diet from mostly processed, refined carbohydrates to whole foods, protein, carbohydrates from fruits and vegetables, and good fats.

PALEO MADE SIMPLE

1. Eat whole foods, not processed

2. Don't eat grains (especially wheat, but also corn, rice, oats, barley)

3. Eliminate dairy products

4. Avoid legumes (beans, peanuts)

5. Enjoy lots of vegetables and plenty of protein

WHAT'S IN THE PALEO PANTRY?

Meats: Bacon, Beef, Buffalo, Lamb, Pork, Veal, Venison

Poultry: Chicken, Duck, Quail, Turkey

Eggs (preferably organic and pasture-raised)

Seafood: Catfish, Clams, Halibut, Herring, Lobster, Mahimahi, Mussels, Salmon, Sardines, Scallops, Shrimp, Trout, Tuna

Fats and Oils: Butter (grass-fed), Coconut oil, Nut oils, Olive oil, Palm oil

Vegetables: Artichokes, Arugula, Asparagus, Broccoli, Brussels sprouts, Cabbage, Carrots, Cauliflower, Celery, Chard, Cucumbers, Eggplant, Fennel, Garlic, Green beans, Kale, Kohlrabi, Leeks, Lettuce, Mushrooms, Onions, Parsnips, Peppers, Radishes, Rutabagas, Spinach, Squash, Sweet potatoes, Tomatoes

Fruits: Apricots, Avocados, Bananas, Blackberries, Blueberries, Cherries, Coconut, Cranberries, Figs, Grapefruit, Grapes, Kiwis, Lemons, Limes, Mangoes, Melons, Nectarines, Oranges, Papayas, Peaches, Pears, Pineapples, Plums, Pomegranates, Raspberries, Rhubarb, Strawberries, Tangerines, Watermelon

Nuts and Seeds: Almonds, Brazil nuts, Hazelnuts, Macadamia nuts, Pecans, Pine nuts, Pistachios, Pumpkin seeds, Sesame seeds, Sunflower seeds, Walnuts

Flavorings: Capers, Coconut aminos, Fresh and dried herbs, Ginger, Lemon and lime juice, Mustard, Vanilla, Vinegars (balsamic, cider, wine), Whole and ground spices

NO PROCESSED FOODS

Grains: Barley, Corn, Oats, Millet, Quinoa, Rice, Rye, Wheat and products containing them or containing gluten

Prepared/Packaged Carbs: Bagels, Baked goods, Biscuits, Breads, Breakfast and snack bars, Cereal, Chips, Cookies, Crackers, Muffins, Pasta, Pretzels, Scones, Taco Shells

Dairy: Cheese, Ice cream, Milk, Yogurt

Legumes: Beans, Chickpeas, Soybeans and soy products, Peanuts

Processed Vegetable Oils: Canola oil, Corn oil, Margarine and "buttery" spreads, Peanut oil, Shortening, Vegetable oil

Sugar and Artificial Sweeteners: Brown, cane and powdered sugar, Corn syrup, Dextrose, Sucrose or products containing them

SO WHAT'S FOR DINNER (AND BREAKFAST AND LUNCH)?

A glance at the Paleo pantry and the many wonderful recipes in this book should give you some good ideas. If you've been eating a typical modern diet of fast food, pasta, bread and sweets, Paleo does take adjustments. You'll spend more time shopping and cooking and being mindful of what you eat—and that's a good thing.

EAT ENOUGH PROTEIN

Meat (especially red meat), poultry and eggs have been maligned for years since they contain cholesterol and saturated fat. They do, but as you have probably noticed, nutritional guidelines change over time. Once egg yolks were forbidden because they raised cholesterol. Then we learned that there are many kinds of cholesterol that your body needs and what we eat may not increase the amount in our bloodstreams. Will eating red meat put you in immediate danger of a heart attack? Not so fast. It depends on what else you're eating, what kind of meat it is and dozens of other factors.

To stick to the Paleo plan you need the simplest, highest quality protein you can find and afford. The best choices are pasture-raised, grass-fed meat and eggs. This is easy to understand if you remember that animals raised on a feedlot and fattened on corn are not remotely like the lean, free-range animals our ancestors consumed.

Pasture-raised meat contains a larger proportion of beneficial omega-3 fatty acids, the same helpful nutrient that is in fish oil and is sadly lacking in the modern diet. When choosing supermarket meat, go for leaner cuts. Most importantly, avoid any processed product that has been "enhanced," marinated or pre-seasoned. Look for eggs from chickens that are fed a diet that increases the content of omega-3s where pasture-raised is hard to find or too expensive.

WHAT'S THE DIFFERENCE BETWEEN PALEO, LOW CARB AND GLUTEN-FREE?

There are similarities, but the basic premise of the Paleo diet is to eat only whole, unprocessed foods. Most low-carb regimens are designed for quick weight loss and require limiting some fruits and vegetables. Gluten-free diets are for those with celiac disease or other sensitivities to the protein in wheat.

CHOOSE HIGH QUALITY SEAFOOD

As with meat, the closer seafood is to its natural state, the better. If you can't go fishing yourself, look for wild-caught fish and purchase from a reputable source that has a high turnover. Pay attention to country of origin when purchasing shrimp. The best choice is U.S. farmed. Imported products can be raised in polluted waters.

ENJOY LOTS OF VEGETABLES AT BREAKFAST, LUNCH AND DINNER

No need to count calories or carbs when it comes to vegetables. It's practically impossible to overeat broccoli or salad greens. Most Paleo diets eliminate potatoes, but sweet potatoes are permitted. (They're botanically unrelated to white potatoes.)

Take this opportunity to try new and different vegetables. How about a frittata with fresh spinach for breakfast? Dress up your lunchtime salad with artichoke hearts. Make crunchy chips from beets or kale for a snack. Roast parsnips, carrots and rutabaga drizzled with olive oil as a side dish. Add fennel, sweet peppers and onions to roast chicken.

SATISFY YOUR SWEET TOOTH WITH FRUIT

Fruit will always taste best and be most nutritious when it is in season. Visit local farmers' markets for great selections. Shopping there may be as close as we can get to hunting and gathering! Remember that fruits contain fructose, which is sugar, and some can be high in carbs. If you're not losing weight and you wish to, try cutting back a little. Be careful of concentrated carbs and sugars in dried fruits and check ingredient lists for hidden sugars.

CHOOSE THE RIGHT KINDS OF FATS

By now you've probably accepted that it's not fat that makes us fat. Our fat storage system is dependent on insulin, and insulin levels increase in response to carbohydrates. Still, the kind of fat we eat does matter. The saturated fat found in red meat used to be considered unhealthy, but that's certainly what Paleo man ate. There were no manufactured vegetable oils.

Did we improve on nature by switching from saturated fat to polyunsaturated vegetable oils? Probably not. What we did do was drastically change the ratio of omega-3 fatty acids to omega-6 fatty acids in our diets. Omega-3s come from grass-fed meats and wild-caught fish. Vegetable oils, including corn, canola and soy, are the primary source of excess omega-6 fatty acids today. This lack of balance is the reason for the increasing interest in fish oil capsules and flaxseed, which are high in omega-3s.

What this means is that you should avoid processed polyunsaturated oils and, of course, trans fats.

COCONUT AMINOS

Made from the sap of the coconut palm, this bottled product can be a replacement for soy sauce. In addition to being made from soy beans, traditional soy sauce also has added wheat, so it contains gluten. Coconut aminos can be used in stir-fries, dressings and wherever you would use soy sauce.

Instead use olive oil, coconut oil or butter from pasture-raised cows. Wherever possible, eat grass-fed meats instead of corn-fed, factory-farmed animals. Keep things interesting with nuts, seeds, herbs and spices.

Making meals and snacks pleasurable doesn't have to mean spending more money or time. Almond or macadamia butter can easily replace peanut butter with your sliced apples. Herbs and spices can add endless variation to the simplest preparations. Herbs and spices are all paleo, but watch ingredient lists if you're purchasing prepared blends. They often contain sugar in some form.

GIVING UP GRAIN

How can wheat, corn, soy, oats, rice and rye be bad for us? They are all domesticated forms of wild grasses that have been managed and "improved" by agriculture for 5,000 years. Remember, that's a short time in terms of human evolution. Wheat, barley and rye contain a protein called gluten. Other grains have similar but somewhat less problematic proteins.

> ### HOW ABOUT WHOLE GRAINS?
> Sorry! While whole grains have a better nutritional profile than refined grains, they contain the same anti-nutrients and can cause the same problems.

Long ago humans lived without grain. Today our diets are dominated by it. We eat a muffin for breakfast, a sandwich for lunch and a bowl of pasta for dinner. There's a lot of hidden gluten, soy and corn in processed foods as well. It's used to improve the texture of everything from hot dogs to ketchup. Corn appears as high fructose corn syrup among other manufactured additives. Soy lurks in snack foods, cooking oils and most dairy replacement products. Start reading labels and you will be stunned at the amount of grain you consume without being aware of it.

GRAINS ARE EASY TO SWALLOW, BUT HARD TO DIGEST

Grain is hard on our digestive system because it contains anti-nutrients. From a plant's perspective these are defensive mechanisms. Plants can't run away from a predator so they evolved chemical protections to make them less attractive as food and to keep them viable. What protects a plant's seeds also protects it from easy digestion, so for humans that makes it an anti-nutrient. One of the many (and most studied) of grains' anti-nutrients is lectin. It occurs in virtually all plants to varying degrees, but is much more concentrated in grain. Lectins are not broken down enough to easily pass into your bloodstream as smaller molecules, so they can compromise the lining of your intestines and cause everything from food intolerances to autoimmune diseases.

WHERE WILL I GET CALCIUM WITHOUT DAIRY?

There are plenty of foods, including dark green leafy vegetables, that supply calcium. More importantly, the body's ability to absorb calcium depends on other nutrients, especially magnesium and vitamin K2, which can come from a variety of vegetable sources. Phytate, an anti-nutrient present in wheat, can also bind with calcium and prevent absorption.

BUT WE NEED CARBS!

Sure we do, but we don't need all the starch and sugar we consume today. We eat a lot more bad carbs than our grandparents did. Carbohydrates are broken down into glucose (sugar) quickly in the bloodstream. If you eat more than you need, your body stores the excess as fat.

There are many sources of good carbs that aren't grain. Fruits and nuts are high in carbohydrates. So are many vegetables including sweet potatoes, carrots and winter squash. They also contribute a wide range of nutrients to your diet.

SAY BYE-BYE TO BEANS

Digesting beans presents most of the same problems as grain. Beans, peanuts (not a nut, but a legume), soybeans and lentils have anti-nutrients just like grains. Like grains, they are difficult to digest. That's why they cause gas. Soaking, fermenting and cooking beans reduces the level of lectins but doesn't remove them. In fact, red kidney beans have such a high concentration of lectin that if they are not thoroughly cooked, they can cause illness.

DON'T DO (MOST) DAIRY

Hunter-gatherers certainly didn't have a herd of milk cows following them around. Most of the dairy products we use are highly processed and come from grain-fed cows. They're ultra-pasteurized, homogenized and then fortified to replace nutrients that have been lost. Skim and reduced-fat milk have more lactose, which is milk sugar, because that's what's left when the fat is removed. Lactose intolerance is common. Butter or cream from pasture-raised animals is usually well tolerated since it contains fewer irritating proteins and almost no lactose.

BUT WE NEED FIBER!

Paleo man consumed a great deal of fiber from wild greens and fruits, not from grains or legumes. Following the Paleo path means eating a lot more fruits and vegetables than our modern, grain-heavy diet provides. You'll be getting fiber from avocados, broccoli, carrots and greens instead of a sweet bran muffin or a processed breakfast cereal.

MAKE PALEO FIT YOUR LIFE AND ENJOY WHAT YOU EAT

A healthy diet is one you can stick with for life and that can be tailored to your tastes and sensitivities. Eating Paleo doesn't require counting calories or carbs. How many meals or snacks you have is up to you. Don't sweat it if you break the rules from time to time. This is not a crash diet. Eat whole, natural foods and enjoy them. If you can't live without cheese or the occasional slice of bread, add them in moderation. Once you experience how good it feels to eat the way evolution intended, the rest is easy.

Page 86

Page 28

SLOW COOKING HINTS AND TIPS

Sizes of CROCK-POT® Slow Cookers

Smaller **CROCK-POT®** slow cookers—such as 1- to 3½-quart models—are the perfect size for cooking for singles, a couple or empty nesters (and also for serving dips).

While medium-size **CROCK-POT®** slow cookers (those holding somewhere between 3 quarts and 5 quarts) will easily cook enough food at a time to feed a small family. They are also convenient for holiday side dishes or appetizers.

Large **CROCK-POT®** slow cookers are great for large family dinners, holiday entertaining and potluck suppers. A 6- to 7-quart model is ideal if you like to make meals in advance, or have dinner tonight and store leftovers for another day.

Types of CROCK-POT® Slow Cookers

Current **CROCK-POT®** slow cookers come equipped with many different features and benefits, from auto cook programs to oven-safe stoneware to timed programming. Please visit **WWW.CROCK-POT.COM** to find the **CROCK-POT®** slow cooker that best suits your needs.

How you plan to use a **CROCK-POT®** slow cooker may affect the model you choose to purchase. For everyday cooking, choose a size large enough to serve your family. If you plan to use the **CROCK-POT®** slow cooker primarily for entertaining, choose one of the larger sizes. Basic **CROCK-POT®** slow cookers can hold as little as 16 ounces or as much as 7 quarts. The smallest sizes are great for keeping dips warm on a buffet, while the larger sizes can more readily fit large quantities of food and larger roasts.

Cooking, Stirring and Food Safety

CROCK-POT® slow cookers are safe to leave unattended. The outer heating base may get hot as it cooks, but it should not pose a fire hazard. The heating element in the heating base functions at a low wattage and is safe for your countertops.

Your **CROCK-POT**® slow cooker should be filled about one-half to three-fourths full for most recipes unless otherwise instructed. Lean meats such as chicken or pork tenderloin will cook faster than meats with more connective tissue and fat such as beef chuck or pork shoulder. Bone-in meats will take longer than boneless cuts. Typical **CROCK-POT**® slow cooker dishes take approximately 7 to 8 hours to reach the simmer point on LOW and about 3 to 4 hours on HIGH. Once the vegetables and meat start to simmer and braise, their flavors will fully blend and meat will become fall-off-the-bone tender.

According to the U.S. Department of Agriculture, all bacteria are killed at a temperature of 165°F. It's important to follow the recommended cooking times and not to open the lid often, especially early in the cooking process when heat is building up inside the unit. If you need to open the lid to check on your food or are adding additional ingredients, remember to allow additional cooking time if necessary to ensure food is cooked through and tender.

Large **CROCK-POT**® slow cookers, the 6- to 7-quart sizes, may benefit from a quick stir halfway through cook time to help distribute heat and promote even cooking. It's usually unnecessary to stir at all, as even ½ cup liquid will help to distribute heat and the stoneware is the perfect medium for holding food at an even temperature throughout the cooking process.

Oven-Safe Stoneware

All **CROCK-POT**® slow cooker removable stoneware inserts may (without their lids) be used safely in ovens at up to 400°F. In addition, all **CROCK-POT**® slow cookers are microwavable without their lids. If you own another slow cooker brand, please refer to your owner's manual for specific stoneware cooking medium tolerances.

Frozen Food

Frozen food can be successfully cooked in a **CROCK-POT**® slow cooker. However, it will require longer cooking time than the same recipe made with fresh food. It is almost always preferable to thaw frozen food prior to placing it in the **CROCK-POT**® slow cooker. Using an instant-read thermometer is recommended to ensure meat is fully cooked through.

Vegetables

Root vegetables often cook more slowly than meat. Cut vegetables accordingly to cook at the same rate as meat—large or small or lean versus marbled—and place near the sides or bottom of the stoneware to facilitate cooking.

Herbs

Fresh herbs add flavor and color when added at the end of the cooking cycle; if added at the beginning, many fresh herbs' flavor will dissipate over long cook times. Ground and/or dried herbs and spices work well in slow cooking and may be added at the beginning of cook time. For dishes with shorter cook times, hearty fresh herbs such as rosemary and thyme hold up well. The flavor power of all herbs and spices can vary greatly depending on their particular strength and shelf life. Use chili powders and garlic powder sparingly, as these can sometimes intensify over the long cook times. Always taste the finished dish and correct seasonings including salt and pepper.

Liquids

It's not necessary to use more than ½ to 1 cup liquid in most instances since juices in meats and vegetables are retained more in slow cooking than in conventional cooking. Excess liquid can be cooked down and concentrated after slow cooking on the stovetop or by setting the **CROCK-POT**® slow cooker to HIGH. Cook, uncovered, on HIGH for approximately 15 minutes or until juices are thickened.

Fish

Fish is delicate and should be stirred into the **CROCK-POT**® slow cooker gently during the last 15 to 30 minutes of cooking time. Cover; cook just until cooked through and serve immediately.

BEEF AND LAMB

Veggie Soup with Beef

MAKES 4 SERVINGS

2 cans (15 ounces *each*) mixed vegetables

1 pound cubed beef stew meat

1 can (8 ounces) tomato sauce

2 cloves garlic, minced

Combine vegetables, beef, tomato sauce and garlic in **CROCK-POT**® slow cooker; stir to blend. Add enough water to fill **CROCK-POT**® slow cooker to within ½ inch of top. Cover; cook on LOW 8 to 10 hours.

Braised Lamb Shanks

MAKES 4 SERVINGS

- 4 **(12- to 16-ounce) lamb shanks**
- ¾ **teaspoon salt, divided**
- ¼ **teaspoon black pepper**
- 1 **tablespoon olive oil**
- 1 **medium onion, chopped**
- 2 **stalks celery, chopped**
- 2 **carrots, chopped**
- 6 **cloves garlic, minced**
- 1 **teaspoon dried basil**
- 1 **can (about 14 ounces) diced tomatoes**
- 2 **tablespoons tomato paste**
- **Chopped fresh Italian parsley (optional)**

1 Coat inside of **CROCK-POT**® slow cooker with nonstick cooking spray. Season lamb with ½ teaspoon salt and pepper. Heat oil in large skillet over medium-high heat. Add lamb; cook 8 to 10 minutes or until browned on all sides. Remove lamb to **CROCK-POT**® slow cooker.

2 Return skillet to medium-high heat. Add onion, celery, carrots, garlic and basil; cook and stir 3 to 4 minutes or until vegetables are softened. Add tomatoes, tomato paste and remaining ¼ teaspoon salt; cook and stir 2 to 3 minutes or until slightly thickened. Pour tomato mixture over lamb shanks in **CROCK-POT**® slow cooker. Garnish with parsley.

CHUCK AND STOUT SOUP

MAKES 6 TO 8 SERVINGS

3 **pounds boneless beef chuck roast, cut into 1-inch cubes**

Salt and black pepper

2 **tablespoons olive oil**

8 **cups beef broth**

3 **onions, thinly sliced**

6 **carrots, diced**

3 **stalks celery, diced**

4 **cloves garlic, minced**

2 **packages (10 ounces *each*) cremini mushrooms, thinly sliced**

1 **package (about 1 ounce) dried porcini mushrooms, processed to a fine powder**

4 **sprigs fresh thyme**

1 **can (12 ounces) stout beer**

Sprigs fresh Italian parsley (optional)

1 Season beef with salt and pepper. Heat oil in large skillet over medium-high heat. Add beef in batches; cook 5 to 7 minutes or until browned on all sides. Remove beef to **CROCK-POT®** slow cooker.

2 Bring broth to a boil in large saucepan over high heat. Reduce heat to low; simmer until reduced by half.

3 Add reduced broth, onions, carrots, celery, garlic, mushrooms, thyme and stout to **CROCK-POT®** slow cooker. Cover; cook on LOW 10 hours or on HIGH 6 hours. Garnish each serving with parsley.

Note: A coffee grinder, food processor or blender works best for processing dried mushrooms.

Pot Roast with Bacon and Mushrooms

MAKES 6 TO 8 SERVINGS

6 slices bacon

1 (2½ to 3-pound) boneless beef chuck roast, trimmed

¾ teaspoon salt, divided

¼ teaspoon black pepper

¾ cup chopped shallots

8 ounces sliced white mushrooms

¼ ounce dried porcini mushrooms (optional)

4 cloves garlic, minced

1 teaspoon dried oregano

1 cup chicken broth

2 tablespoons tomato paste

Roasted Cauliflower (optional)

1 Heat large skillet over medium heat. Add bacon; cook 7 to 8 minutes until crisp-cooked and tender. Remove to large paper towel-lined plate; crumble.

2 Pour off all but 2 tablespoons fat from skillet. Season roast with ½ teaspoon salt and pepper. Heat skillet over medium-high heat. Add roast; cook 8 minutes or until well browned. Remove to large plate. Add shallots, white mushrooms, porcini mushrooms, if desired, garlic, oregano and remaining ¼ teaspoon salt; cook 3 to 4 minutes or until softened. Remove shallot mixture to **CROCK-POT**® slow cooker.

3 Stir bacon into **CROCK-POT**® slow cooker. Place roast on top of vegetables. Combine broth and tomato paste in small bowl; stir to blend. Pour broth mixture over roast. Cover; cook on LOW 8 hours. Remove roast to large cutting board. Let stand 10 minutes before slicing. Top with vegetables and cooking liquid. Serve with Roasted Cauliflower, if desired.

Roasted Cauliflower: Preheat oven to 375°F. Break cauliflower into florets; coat with olive oil. Roast 20 minutes. Turn; roast 15 minutes. Makes 6 servings.

Beef and Beet Borscht

MAKES 6 TO 8 SERVINGS

6 slices bacon

1 boneless beef chuck roast (1½ pounds), trimmed and cut into ½-inch pieces

1 medium onion, chopped

4 cloves garlic, minced

4 medium beets, peeled and cut into ½-inch pieces

2 large carrots, sliced

3 cups beef broth

6 sprigs fresh dill

3 tablespoons honey

3 tablespoons red wine vinegar

2 whole bay leaves

3 cups shredded green cabbage

1 Heat large skillet over medium heat. Add bacon; cook and stir until crisp. Remove to paper towel-lined plate using slotted spoon; crumble.

2 Return skillet to medium-high heat. Add beef; cook 5 minutes or until browned. Remove beef to **CROCK-POT**® slow cooker.

3 Pour off all but 1 tablespoon fat from skillet. Add onion and garlic; cook 4 minutes or until onion is softened. Remove onion mixture to **CROCK-POT**® slow cooker. Stir in beets, carrots, broth, bacon, dill, honey, vinegar and bay leaves. Cover; cook on LOW 5 to 6 hours. Stir in cabbage. Cover; cook on LOW 30 minutes. Remove and discard bay leaves before serving.

BEEF AND VEAL MEAT LOAF

MAKES 6 SERVINGS

1 tablespoon olive oil

1 small onion, chopped

½ red bell pepper, chopped

3 cloves garlic, minced

1 teaspoon dried oregano

1 pound ground beef

1 pound ground veal

1 egg

3 tablespoons tomato paste

1 teaspoon salt

½ teaspoon black pepper

1 Coat inside of **CROCK-POT®** slow cooker with nonstick cooking spray. Heat oil in large skillet over medium-high heat. Add onion, bell pepper, garlic and oregano; cook and stir 5 minutes until vegetables are softened. Remove onion mixture to large bowl; cool 6 minutes.

2 Add beef, veal, egg, tomato paste, salt and black pepper; mix well. Form into 9×5-inch loaf; place in **CROCK-POT®** slow cooker. Cover; cook on LOW 5 to 6 hours. Remove meatloaf to large cutting board; let stand 10 minutes before slicing.

Sauvignon Blanc Beef with Beets and Thyme

MAKES 6 SERVINGS

1 pound red or yellow beets, scrubbed and quartered

2 tablespoons extra virgin olive oil

1 boneless beef chuck roast (about 3 pounds)*

1 medium yellow onion, peeled and quartered

2 cloves garlic, minced

5 sprigs fresh thyme

1 whole bay leaf

2 whole cloves

2 cups chicken broth

2 tablespoons tomato paste

Salt and black pepper

*Unless you have a 5-, 6- or 7-quart **CROCK-POT**® slow cooker, cut any roast larger than 2½ pounds in half so it cooks completely.

1 Layer beets evenly in **CROCK-POT**® slow cooker.

2 Heat oil in large skillet over medium heat. Brown roast on all sides 4 to 5 minutes. Add onion and garlic during last few minutes of browning. Remove to **CROCK-POT**® slow cooker.

3 Add thyme, bay leaf and cloves to **CROCK-POT**® slow cooker. Combine broth and tomato paste in medium bowl. Season broth mixture with salt and pepper; mix well to combine. Pour over roast and beets in **CROCK-POT**® slow cooker. Cover; cook on LOW 8 to 10 hours or until roast is fork-tender and beets are tender. Remove and discard bay leaf before serving.

Braised Fruited Lamb

MAKES 6 TO 8 SERVINGS

6 **tablespoons extra virgin olive oil**

4 **pounds lamb shanks**

2 **tablespoons salt**

2 **tablespoons black pepper**

1 **cup dried apricots**

1 **cup dried figs**

1½ **cups water**

½ **cup white vinegar**

¼ **cup raspberry jam**

½ **teaspoon ground allspice**

½ **teaspoon ground cinnamon**

1 Preheat broiler. Brush oil on lamb shanks; season with salt and pepper. Place shanks on large baking sheet; broil 5 minutes per side. Remove to **CROCK-POT**® slow cooker. Add dried fruits.

2 Combine water, vinegar, jam, allspice and cinnamon in small bowl. Pour over lamb shanks. Cover; cook on LOW 8 to 9 hours or on HIGH 4 to 5 hours.

Brisket with Sweet Onions

MAKES 10 SERVINGS

2 **large sweet onions, cut into 10 (½-inch) slices***

1 **flat-cut boneless beef brisket (about 3½ pounds)**

  Salt and black pepper

2 **cans (about 14 ounces *each*) beef broth**

1 **teaspoon cracked black peppercorns**

*Preferably Maui, Vidalia or Walla Walla onions.

1 Coat inside of **CROCK-POT**® slow cooker with nonstick cooking spray. Line bottom with onion slices.

2 Season brisket with salt and pepper, if desired. Heat large skillet over medium-high heat. Add brisket; cook 10 to 12 minutes or until browned on all sides. Remove to **CROCK-POT**® slow cooker.

3 Pour broth into **CROCK-POT**® slow cooker. Sprinkle brisket with peppercorns. Cover; cook on HIGH 5 to 7 hours.

4 Remove brisket to cutting board. Cover loosely with foil; let stand 10 to 15 minutes. Slice evenly against the grain into ten slices. To serve, arrange onions on serving platter and spread slices of brisket on top. Serve with cooking liquid.

Tip: Use freshly ground pepper as a quick and simple flavor enhancer for **CROCK-POT**® slow cooker dishes.

Hearty Beef Short Ribs

MAKES 6 TO 8 SERVINGS

2½ **pounds beef flanken-style short ribs, bone-in**

1 **to 2 tablespoons coarse salt**

1 **to 2 tablespoons black pepper**

2 **tablespoons olive oil, divided**

2 **carrots, diced**

2 **stalks celery, diced**

1 **large yellow onion, diced**

3 **cloves garlic, minced**

3 **whole bay leaves**

⅓ **cup beef broth**

⅓ **cup crushed tomatoes**

⅓ **cup balsamic vinegar**

Carrot slices, cooked (optional)

1 Season ribs with salt and black pepper. Drizzle with 1 tablespoon oil. Heat remaining 1 tablespoon oil in large skillet. Cook ribs 2 to 3 minutes per side or until just browned. Remove ribs to **CROCK-POT**® slow cooker. Add diced carrots, celery, onion, garlic and bay leaves.

2 Combine broth, tomatoes and vinegar in small bowl. Season with salt and black pepper, if desired. Pour mixture into **CROCK-POT**® slow cooker. Cover; cook on LOW 8 to 9 hours or on HIGH 5½ to 6 hours, turning once or twice, until meat is tender and falling off the bone.

3 Remove ribs to serving platter. Remove and discard bay leaves. Process sauce in food processor or blender to desired consistency. Pour sauce over ribs. Serve with sliced carrots, if desired.

Tip: For a change of pace from ordinary short rib recipes, ask your butcher for flanken-style beef short ribs. Flanken-style ribs are cut across the bones into wide, flat portions. They provide all the meaty flavor of the more common English-style short ribs with smaller, more manageable bones.

Braised Lamb Shank Osso Buco

MAKES 4 SERVINGS

4 **teaspoons olive oil, divided**

4 **lamb shanks (about 12 to 16 ounces *each*), trimmed**

¾ **teaspoon salt, divided**

½ **teaspoon black pepper, divided**

1 **large onion, chopped**

4 **cloves garlic, minced**

½ **cup dry red wine**

1 **can (about 14 ounces) Italian seasoned diced tomatoes**

½ **cup chopped fresh basil**

1 Heat 2 teaspoons oil in large skillet over medium-high heat. Sprinkle lamb with ½ teaspoon salt and ¼ teaspoon pepper. Add to skillet; cook 8 to 10 minutes or until browned on all sides, turning occasionally. Remove to **CROCK-POT**® slow cooker.

2 Heat remaining 2 teaspoons oil in same skillet over medium heat. Add onion and garlic; cook and stir 1 minute or until starting to soften. Pour in wine. Bring to a boil; cook 2 minutes. Add tomatoes; cook 4 minutes. Remove to **CROCK-POT**® slow cooker. Cover; cook on LOW 5 to 6 hours or until meat is tender.

3 Stir in basil and remaining ¼ teaspoon salt and ¼ teaspoon pepper.

KICK'N CHILI

MAKES 6 SERVINGS

2 **pounds ground beef**

2 **cloves garlic, minced**

1 **tablespoon** *each* **salt, ground cumin, chili powder, paprika, dried oregano and black pepper**

2 **teaspoons red pepper flakes**

¼ **teaspoon ground red pepper**

1 **tablespoon vegetable oil**

3 **cans (about 14 ounces** *each***) diced tomatoes with mild green chiles**

1 **jar (16 ounces) salsa**

1 **onion, chopped**

1 Combine beef, garlic, salt, cumin, chili powder, paprika, oregano, black pepper, red pepper flakes and ground red pepper in large bowl.

2 Heat oil in large skillet over medium-high heat. Brown beef 6 to 8 minutes, stirring to break up meat. Drain fat. Add tomatoes, salsa and onion; mix well. Remove to **CROCK-POT**® slow cooker. Cover; cook on LOW 4 to 6 hours.

Tip: This chunky chili is perfect for the spicy food lover in your family. Reduce the red pepper flakes for a milder flavor.

CORNED BEEF AND CABBAGE

MAKES 6 SERVINGS

1 head cabbage (about 1½ pounds), cut into 6 wedges

4 ounces baby carrots

1 corned beef (about 3 pounds), with seasoning packet (perforate packet with knife tip)*

4 cups water

⅓ cup prepared mustard

⅓ cup honey

*Unless you have a 5-, 6- or 7-quart **CROCK-POT®** slow cooker, cut any roast larger than 2½ pounds in half so it cooks completely.

1 Place cabbage and carrots in **CROCK-POT®** slow cooker. Place seasoning packet on top. Add corned beef, fat side up. Pour in water. Cover; cook on LOW 10 hours.

2 Remove and discard seasoning packet. Combine mustard and honey in small bowl; stir to blend. Remove beef to cutting board and slice. Serve with vegetables and mustard sauce.

Cajun Pot Roast

MAKES 6 SERVINGS

1 boneless beef chuck roast (3 pounds)

1 to 2 tablespoons Cajun seasoning

1 tablespoon vegetable oil

1 can (about 14 ounces) diced tomatoes

1 can (about 14 ounces) diced tomatoes with mild green chiles

1 medium onion, chopped

1 cup chopped rutabaga

1 cup chopped mushrooms

1 cup chopped turnip

1 cup chopped parsnip

1 cup chopped green bell pepper

1 cup green beans

1 cup sliced carrots

1 cup corn

2 tablespoons hot pepper sauce

1 teaspoon sugar

½ teaspoon black pepper

¾ cup water

1 Coat inside of **CROCK-POT®** slow cooker with nonstick cooking spray. Season roast with cajun seasoning. Heat oil in large skillet over medium-high heat. Brown roast 5 minutes on each side.

2 Place roast, tomatoes, onion, rutabaga, mushrooms, turnip, parsnip, bell pepper, beans, carrots, corn, hot pepper sauce, sugar and black pepper in **CROCK-POT®** slow cooker. Pour in water. Cover; cook on LOW 6 hours.

Portuguese Beef Shanks

MAKES 4 SERVINGS

4 **cloves garlic, minced**

1 **large white onion, diced**

1 **green bell pepper, diced**

2 **jalapeño peppers, seeded and minced***

½ **cup diced celery**

½ **cup minced fresh Italian parsley**

4 **medium beef shanks, bone in (about 3 pounds total)**

1 **tablespoon fresh rosemary, minced**

1 **teaspoon salt**

2 **cups beef broth**

Horseradish sauce (optional)

*Jalapeño peppers can sting and irritate the skin, so wear rubber gloves when handling peppers and do not touch your eyes.

1 Place garlic, onion, bell pepper, jalapeño peppers, celery and parsley in **CROCK-POT®** slow cooker.

2 Rub beef shanks with rosemary and salt. Place shanks on top of vegetables. Pour broth over shanks and vegetables. Cover; cook on LOW 7 to 9 hours.

3 Spoon vegetable sauce over shanks. Serve with horseradish sauce, if desired.

BRAISED SHORT RIBS WITH AROMATIC SPICES

MAKES 4 SERVINGS

1 **tablespoon olive oil**

3 **pounds bone-in beef short ribs, trimmed**

1 **teaspoon ground cumin, divided**

1 **teaspoon salt, divided**

½ **teaspoon black pepper, divided**

2 **medium onions, halved and thinly sliced**

10 **cloves garlic, thinly sliced**

2 **tablespoons balsamic vinegar**

2 **tablespoons honey**

1 **cinnamon stick**

2 **star anise pods**

2 **large sweet potatoes, peeled and cut into ¾-inch cubes**

1 **cup beef broth**

1 Heat oil in large skillet over medium-high heat. Season ribs with ½ teaspoon cumin, ¾ teaspoon salt and ¼ teaspoon pepper. Add to skillet; cook 8 minutes or until browned, turning occasionally. Remove ribs to large plate.

2 Heat same skillet over medium heat. Add onions and garlic; cook 12 to 14 minutes or until onions are lightly browned. Stir in vinegar; cook 1 minute. Add remaining ½ teaspoon cumin, ¼ teaspoon salt, ¼ teaspoon pepper, honey, cinnamon stick and star anise; cook and stir 30 seconds. Remove mixture to **CROCK-POT**® slow cooker. Stir in potatoes; top with ribs. Pour in broth.

3 Cover; cook on LOW 8 to 9 hours or until meat is falling off the bones. Remove and discard bones from ribs. Skim fat from surface of sauce. Serve meat with sauce and vegetables.

Tomato and Red Wine Brisket

MAKES 8 SERVINGS

3 **to 3½ pounds beef brisket, trimmed**

¾ **teaspoon salt, divided**

¼ **teaspoon black pepper**

1 **tablespoon olive oil**

1 **large red onion, sliced**

½ **cup dry red wine**

1 **can (28 ounces) diced tomatoes with basil, oregano and garlic**

1 Coat inside of **CROCK-POT**® slow cooker with nonstick cooking spray. Season beef with ½ teaspoon salt and pepper. Heat oil in large skillet over medium-high heat. Add beef; cook 5 minutes per side until browned. Remove to **CROCK-POT**® slow cooker.

2 Return skillet to medium-high heat. Add onion; cook and stir 5 minutes or until softened. Pour in wine. Bring mixture to a boil, scraping up any browned bits from bottom of skillet. Cook 3 to 4 minutes until mixture nearly evaporates. Stir in tomatoes. Bring to a boil; cook 6 to 7 minutes or until slightly thickened. Stir in remaining ¼ teaspoon salt. Pour mixture over beef in **CROCK-POT**® slow cooker.

3 Cover; cook on LOW 7 to 8 hours. Remove beef to large cutting board. Cover loosely with foil; let stand 15 minutes before slicing. Turn **CROCK-POT**® slow cooker to HIGH. Cook, uncovered, on HIGH 10 minutes or until sauce is thickened. Serve sauce over brisket.

Braised Chipotle Beef

MAKES 4 TO 6 SERVINGS

- **3 pounds boneless beef chuck roast, cut into 2-inch pieces**
- **1½ teaspoons salt, plus additional for seasoning**
- **½ teaspoon black pepper, plus additional for seasoning**
- **3 tablespoons vegetable oil, divided**
- **1 large onion, cut into 1-inch pieces**
- **2 red bell peppers, cut into 1-inch pieces**
- **3 tablespoons tomato paste**
- **1 tablespoon minced garlic**
- **1 tablespoon chipotle chili powder***
- **1 tablespoon paprika**
- **1 tablespoon ground cumin**
- **1 teaspoon dried oregano**
- **1 cup beef broth**
- **1 can (about 14 ounces) diced tomatoes, drained**

*Or substitute conventional chili powder.

1 Pat beef dry with paper towels and season with salt and black pepper. Heat 2 tablespoons oil in large skillet over medium-high heat. Working in batches, cook beef in skillet, turning to brown all sides. Remove each batch to **CROCK-POT**® slow cooker as it is finished.

2 Return skillet to medium-high heat. Add remaining 1 tablespoon oil. Add onion; cook and stir just until softened. Add bell peppers; cook 2 minutes. Stir in tomato paste, garlic, chili powder, paprika, cumin, 1½ teaspoons salt, oregano and ½ teaspoon black pepper; cook and stir 1 minute. Remove to **CROCK-POT**® slow cooker.

3 Return skillet to heat; add broth. Cook, stirring to scrape up any browned bits from bottom of skillet. Pour over beef in **CROCK-POT**® slow cooker. Stir in tomatoes. Cover; cook on LOW 7 hours. Turn off heat. Let cooking liquid stand 5 minutes. Skim off and discard fat. Serve beef with cooking liquid.

Sauerbraten

MAKES 5 SERVINGS

1 boneless beef rump roast (1¼ pounds)

3 cups baby carrots

1½ cups fresh or frozen pearl onions

¼ cup raisins

½ cup water

½ cup red wine vinegar

1 tablespoon honey

½ teaspoon salt

½ teaspoon dry mustard

½ teaspoon garlic-pepper seasoning

¼ teaspoon ground cloves

1 Heat large nonstick skillet over medium-high heat. Brown roast on all sides, turning as it browns. Place roast, carrots, onions and raisins in **CROCK-POT**® slow cooker.

2 Combine water, vinegar, honey, salt, mustard, garlic-pepper seasoning and cloves in large bowl; mix well. Pour mixture over meat and vegetables in **CROCK-POT**® slow cooker. Cover; cook on LOW 4 to 6 hours.

3 Remove roast to large cutting board. Cover loosely with foil; let stand 10 to 15 minutes before slicing. Serve meat with vegetables and cooking liquid.

Deep Dark Black Coffee'd Beef

MAKES 6 SERVINGS

2 **cups sliced mushrooms**

1 **cup chopped onions**

2 **teaspoons instant coffee granules**

1½ **teaspoons chili powder**

½ **teaspoon black pepper**

1 **lean boneless beef chuck roast (about 2 pounds)**

1 **tablespoon vegetable oil**

½ **cup water**

1 **tablespoon Worcestershire sauce**

1 **teaspoon beef bouillon granules or 1 cube beef bouillon**

½ **teaspoon garlic powder**

Hot cooked asparagus (optional)

1 Coat inside of **CROCK-POT®** slow cooker with nonstick cooking spray. Add mushrooms and onions.

2 Combine coffee granules, chili powder and pepper in small bowl; stir to blend. Rub evenly onto beef. Heat oil in large skillet over medium-high heat. Add beef; cook 3 minutes per side or until browned. Place beef on vegetables in **CROCK-POT®** slow cooker.

3 Add water, Worcestershire sauce, bouillon granules and garlic powder. Cover; cook on LOW 8 hours or HIGH 4 hours.

4 Remove beef to large serving platter. Pour cooking liquid through fine-mesh sieve to drain well, reserving liquid and vegetables. Place vegetables over beef. Allow cooking liquid to stand 2 to 3 minutes. Skim and discard excess fat. Serve with remaining liquid and asparagus, if desired.

Tip: "Au jus" means "with juice," and usually refers to the cooking liquid in which meats have cooked. If you prefer a thicker sauce, blend 1 tablespoon cornstarch and 2 tablespoons water. Whisk into the cooking liquid and continue cooking until it thickens.

MIDDLE EASTERN BEEF AND EGGPLANT STEW

MAKES 4 SERVINGS

1 teaspoon olive oil

1 small eggplant, trimmed and cut into 1-inch chunks

2 cups shiitake or cremini mushrooms, quartered

1 can (about 14 ounces) diced tomatoes

½ pound boneless beef top round steak, cut into 1-inch pieces

1 medium onion, chopped

1 cup beef broth

1 clove garlic, minced

½ teaspoon salt

⅓ teaspoon ground cumin

¼ teaspoon red pepper flakes

¼ teaspoon ground cinnamon

Grated peel of 1 lemon

⅛ teaspoon black pepper

1 Heat oil in large nonstick skillet over medium-high heat. Add eggplant; cook 3 to 5 minutes or until lightly browned on all sides, stirring frequently. Remove eggplant to **CROCK-POT®** slow cooker.

2 Stir in all remaining ingredients. Cover; cook on LOW 6 hours.

Mom's Brisket

MAKES 4 SERVINGS

4 teaspoons paprika, divided

1 beef brisket (about 2 pounds), scored on both sides

Olive oil

2 cups water

1½ cups ketchup

2 large onions, diced

2 tablespoons horseradish

4 Yukon Gold potatoes, peeled and cut into 1-inch pieces

2 teaspoons paprika

Kosher salt and black pepper

1 Rub 2 teaspoons paprika evenly over beef. Heat oil in large skillet over medium heat. Brown brisket on both sides. Remove to **CROCK-POT**® slow cooker.

2 Combine water, ketchup, onions and horseradish in small bowl; stir to blend. Add to **CROCK-POT**® slow cooker. Cover; cook on LOW 7 to 9 hours or on HIGH 3 to 5 hours.

3 Remove meat to large cutting board. Cool and cut in thin diagonal slices. (At this point, meat can be refrigerated overnight.)

4 Sprinkle potatoes with remaining 2 teaspoons paprika. Place in **CROCK-POT**® slow cooker. Place sliced meat on top of potatoes. Season with salt and pepper. Cover; cook on LOW 6 to 8 hours or on HIGH 3 to 4 hours.

PLEASING PORK

Harvest Ham Supper

MAKES 6 SERVINGS

6 carrots, cut into 2-inch pieces

3 medium sweet potatoes, quartered

1 boneless ham (1 to 1½ pounds)

1 cup maple syrup

1 Arrange carrots and sweet potatoes in bottom of **CROCK-POT**® slow cooker.

2 Place ham on top of vegetables. Pour syrup over ham and vegetables. Cover; cook on LOW 6 to 8 hours.

MEDITERRANEAN MEATBALL RATATOUILLE

MAKES 6 SERVINGS

1 **pound bulk mild Italian sausage**

1 **package (8 ounces) sliced mushrooms**

1 **small eggplant, diced**

1 **zucchini, diced**

½ **cup chopped yellow onion**

1 **clove garlic, minced**

1 **teaspoon dried oregano**

1 **teaspoon salt**

½ **teaspoon black pepper**

2 **tomatoes, diced**

1 **tablespoon tomato paste**

2 **tablespoons chopped fresh basil**

1 **teaspoon fresh lemon juice**

1 Shape sausage into 1-inch meatballs. Brown meatballs in large skillet over medium heat. Place half the meatballs in **CROCK-POT**® slow cooker. Add half each of mushrooms, eggplant and zucchini. Top with onion, garlic, ½ teaspoon oregano, ½ teaspoon salt and ¼ teaspoon pepper.

2 Add remaining meatballs, mushrooms, eggplant, zucchini, ½ teaspoon oregano, ½ teaspoon salt and ¼ teaspoon pepper. Cover; cook on LOW 6 to 7 hours.

3 Stir diced tomatoes and tomato paste into **CROCK-POT**® slow cooker. Cover; cook on LOW 15 minutes. Stir in basil and lemon juice just before serving.

Boneless Pork Roast with Garlic

MAKES 4 TO 6 SERVINGS

1 boneless pork rib roast (2 to 2½ pounds)

Salt and black pepper

3 tablespoons olive oil, divided

4 cloves garlic, minced

¼ cup chopped fresh rosemary

½ lemon, cut into ⅛- to ¼-inch slices

¾ cup chicken broth

1 Season pork with salt and pepper. Combine 2 tablespoons oil, garlic and rosemary in small bowl. Rub over pork. Roll and tie pork with kitchen string. Tuck lemon slices under string and into ends of roast.

2 Heat remaining 1 tablespoon oil in skillet over medium heat. Add pork; cook 6 to 8 minutes or until browned on all sides. Remove to **CROCK-POT®** slow cooker.

3 Return skillet to heat. Add broth, scraping up any browned bits from bottom of skillet. Pour over pork in **CROCK-POT®** slow cooker. Cover; cook on LOW 8 to 9 hours or on HIGH 3½ to 4 hours.

4 Remove roast to large cutting board. Cover loosely with foil; let stand 10 to 15 minutes before removing kitchen string and slicing. Pour pan juices over sliced pork to serve.

Pulled Pork with Honey-Chipotle Barbecue Sauce

MAKES 8 SERVINGS

1 **tablespoon chili powder, divided**

1 **teaspoon ground chipotle chili, divided**

1 **teaspoon ground cumin, divided**

1 **teaspoon garlic powder, divided**

1 **teaspoon salt**

1 **bone-in pork shoulder, trimmed (3½ pounds)***

1 **can (15 ounces) tomato sauce**

5 **tablespoons honey, divided**

*Unless you have a 5-, 6- or 7-quart **CROCK-POT**® slow cooker, cut any roast larger than 2½ pounds in half so it cooks completely.

1 Coat inside of **CROCK-POT**® slow cooker with nonstick cooking spray. Combine 1 teaspoon chili powder, ½ teaspoon chipotle chili, ½ teaspoon cumin, ½ teaspoon garlic powder and salt in small bowl. Rub pork with chili powder mixture. Place pork in **CROCK-POT**® slow cooker.

2 Combine tomato sauce, 4 tablespoons honey, remaining 2 teaspoons chili powder, ½ teaspoon chipotle chili, ½ teaspoon cumin and ½ teaspoon garlic powder in large bowl. Pour tomato mixture over pork in **CROCK-POT**® slow cooker. Cover; cook on LOW 8 hours.

3 Remove pork to large bowl; cover with foil. Turn **CROCK-POT**® slow cooker to HIGH. Cover; cook on HIGH 30 minutes or until sauce is thickened. Stir in remaining 1 tablespoon honey.

4 Remove bone from pork and discard. Shred pork using two forks. Stir shredded pork into **CROCK-POT**® slow cooker to coat well with sauce.

Spicy Citrus Pork
with Pineapple Salsa

MAKES 12 SERVINGS

1 **tablespoon ground cumin**

½ **teaspoon salt**

1 **teaspoon black pepper**

3 **pounds center-cut pork loin, rinsed and patted dry**

2 **tablespoons vegetable oil**

4 **cans (8 ounces *each*) pineapple tidbits in own juice, drained, ½ cup juice reserved***

3 **tablespoons lemon juice, divided**

2 **teaspoons grated lemon peel**

1 **cup finely chopped orange or red bell pepper**

4 **tablespoons finely chopped red onion**

2 **tablespoons chopped fresh cilantro or mint**

1 **teaspoon grated fresh ginger (optional)**

¼ **teaspoon red pepper flakes (optional)**

*If tidbits are unavailable, purchase pineapple chunks and coarsely chop.

1 Coat inside of **CROCK-POT**® slow cooker with nonstick cooking spray. Combine cumin, salt and black pepper in small bowl. Rub evenly onto pork. Heat oil in medium skillet over medium-high heat. Brown pork loin on all sides 1 to 2 minutes per side. Remove to **CROCK-POT**® slow cooker.

2 Spoon 4 tablespoons of reserved pineapple juice and 2 tablespoons lemon juice over pork. Cover; cook on LOW 2 to 2¼ hours or on HIGH 1 hour and 10 minutes or until meat is tender.

3 Meanwhile, combine pineapple, remaining 4 tablespoons pineapple juice, remaining 1 tablespoon lemon juice, lemon peel, bell pepper, onion, cilantro, ginger, if desired, and red pepper flakes, if desired, in medium bowl. Toss gently and blend well; set aside.

4 Remove pork to cutting board. Cover loosely with foil; let stand 10 to 15 minutes before slicing. Arrange pork slices on serving platter. Pour sauce evenly over slices. Serve salsa on the side.

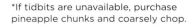

KNOCKWURST AND CABBAGE

MAKES 8 SERVINGS

2 **tablespoons olive oil**

8 **to 10 knockwurst sausage links**

1 **head red cabbage, cut into ¼-inch slices**

½ **cup thinly sliced white onion**

2 **teaspoons caraway seeds**

1 **teaspoon salt**

4 **cups chicken broth**

Chopped fresh Italian parsley (optional)

1 Heat oil in large skillet over medium heat. Cook sausages 5 to 7 minutes until browned on all sides. Remove to **CROCK-POT®** slow cooker.

2 Add cabbage and onion to **CROCK-POT®** slow cooker. Sprinkle with caraway seeds and salt. Add broth. Cover; cook on LOW 4 hours or on HIGH 2 hours. Garnish with parsley.

SWEET AND SPICY PORK PICADILLO

MAKES 4 SERVINGS

1 tablespoon olive oil

1 yellow onion, cut into ¼-inch pieces

2 cloves garlic, minced

1 pound boneless pork country-style ribs, trimmed and cut into 1-inch cubes

1 can (about 14 ounces) diced tomatoes

3 tablespoons cider vinegar

2 canned chipotle peppers in adobo sauce, chopped*

½ cup raisins

½ teaspoon ground cumin

½ teaspoon ground cinnamon

*You may substitute dried chipotle peppers, soaked in warm water about 20 minutes to soften before chopping.

1 Heat oil in large skillet over medium-low heat. Add onion and garlic; cook and stir 4 minutes. Add pork; cook and stir 5 to 7 minutes or until browned. Remove to **CROCK-POT®** slow cooker.

2 Combine tomatoes, vinegar, chipotle peppers, raisins, cumin and cinnamon in medium bowl. Pour over pork in **CROCK-POT®** slow cooker. Cover; cook on LOW 5 hours or on HIGH 3 hours. Remove pork to cutting board; shred with two forks.

Pork Roast with Dijon Tarragon Glaze

MAKES 4 TO 6 SERVINGS

1½ **to 2 pounds boneless pork loin, trimmed**

1 **teaspoon ground paprika**

½ **teaspoon black pepper**

⅓ **cup chicken or vegetable broth**

2 **tablespoons Dijon mustard**

2 **tablespoons lemon juice**

1 **teaspoon minced fresh tarragon**

1 Sprinkle pork with paprika and pepper. Place pork in **CROCK-POT®** slow cooker. Combine broth, mustard, lemon juice and tarragon in small bowl; spoon over pork. Cover; cook on LOW 6 to 8 hours or on HIGH 3 to 4 hours.

2 Remove roast to large cutting board. Let stand 10 to 15 minutes before slicing. Serve with cooking liquid.

Savory Slow Cooker Pork Roast

MAKES 8 SERVINGS

1 **boneless pork blade roast (3 to 4 pounds)***

Salt and black pepper

2 **tablespoons vegetable oil**

1 **medium onion, sliced in ¼-inch-thick rings**

2 **to 3 cloves garlic, chopped**

1 **can (about 15 ounces) chicken broth**

Sprigs fresh oregano (optional)

*Unless you have a 5-, 6- or 7-quart **CROCK-POT®** slow cooker, cut any roast larger than 2½ pounds in half so it cooks completely.

1 Season pork with salt and pepper. Heat oil in large skillet over medium heat; brown roast on all sides.

2 Place onion slices on bottom of **CROCK-POT®** slow cooker; sprinkle with garlic. Place roast on onions; pour broth over roast.

3 Cover; cook on LOW 10 hours or on HIGH 6 to 7 hours. Garnish with oregano.

Pork Roast with Fruit Medley

MAKES 8 SERVINGS

1 **boneless pork loin roast (about 4 pounds)***

1 **tablespoon black pepper**

2 **teaspoons salt**

Nonstick cooking spray

2 **cups green grapes**

1 **cup dried apricots**

1 **cup dried prunes**

2 **whole bay leaves**

1 **teaspoon dried thyme**

2 **cloves garlic, minced**

1 **cup dry red wine**

Juice of ½ lemon

*Unless you have a 5-, 6- or 7-quart **CROCK-POT®** slow cooker, cut any roast larger than 2½ pounds in half so it cooks completely.

1 Season pork with pepper and salt. Spray large skillet with cooking spray; heat over medium-high heat. Add pork; cook 5 to 7 minutes or until browned on all sides.

2 Combine grapes, apricots, prunes, bay leaves, thyme, garlic, wine and lemon juice in **CROCK-POT®** slow cooker; stir to blend. Add pork to **CROCK-POT®** slow cooker; turn to coat. Cover; cook on LOW 7 to 9 hours or on HIGH 3 to 5 hours. Remove and discard bay leaves. Remove roast to cutting board. Cut roast evenly into eight pieces.

Pork Roast with Currant Cherry Salsa

MAKES 8 SERVINGS

1½ **teaspoons chili powder**

¾ **teaspoon salt**

½ **teaspoon garlic powder**

½ **teaspoon paprika**

¼ **teaspoon ground allspice**

1 **boneless pork loin roast (2 pounds)**

Nonstick cooking spray

½ **cup water**

1 **package (1 pound) frozen pitted dark cherries, thawed, drained and halved**

¼ **cup currants or dark raisins**

1 **teaspoon grated orange peel**

1 **teaspoon balsamic vinegar**

⅛ **to ¼ teaspoon red pepper flakes**

1 Combine chili powder, salt, garlic powder, paprika and allspice in small bowl; stir to blend. Rub roast evenly with spice mixture, pressing spices into roast.

2 Spray large skillet with cooking spray; heat over medium-high heat. Add roast; cook 6 to 8 minutes or until browned on all sides. Remove to **CROCK-POT®** slow cooker.

3 Pour water into skillet, stirring to scrape up any brown bits from bottom of skillet. Pour liquid into **CROCK-POT®** slow cooker around roast. Cover; cook on LOW 6 to 8 hours.

4 Remove roast to large cutting board. Cover loosely with foil; let stand 10 to 15 minutes. Strain juices from **CROCK-POT®** slow cooker; discard solids. Keep warm.

5 Turn **CROCK-POT®** slow cooker to HIGH. Add cherries, currants, orange peel, vinegar and red pepper flakes to **CROCK-POT®** slow cooker. Cover; cook on HIGH 30 minutes. Slice pork; spoon warm juices over meat. Serve with salsa.

Asian Pork Tenderloin

MAKES 4 SERVINGS

½ **cup bottled garlic ginger sauce**

¼ **cup sliced green onions**

1 **pork tenderloin (about 1 pound)**

1 **large red onion, cut into slices**

1 **medium red bell pepper, cut into 1-inch pieces**

1 **medium zucchini, cut into ¼-inch slices**

1 **tablespoon olive oil**

1 Combine sauce and green onions in large resealable food storage bag. Add pork. Seal bag; turn to coat. Place bag on large baking sheet; refrigerate 30 minutes or overnight.

2 Combine red onion, bell pepper, zucchini and oil in large bowl; toss to coat. Place vegetables in **CROCK-POT**® slow cooker. Remove pork from bag; place on top of vegetables. Discard marinade. Cover; cook on LOW 6 to 7 hours or on HIGH 4 to 5 hours.

3 Remove pork to large cutting board. Cover loosely with foil; let stand 10 to 15 minutes before slicing. Serve pork with vegetables.

Maple-Dry Rubbed Ribs

MAKES 4 SERVINGS

2 **teaspoons chili powder, divided**

1 **teaspoon ground coriander**

1 **teaspoon garlic powder, divided**

½ **teaspoon salt**

¼ **teaspoon black pepper**

3 **to 3½ pounds pork baby back ribs, trimmed and cut in half**

3 **tablespoons maple syrup, divided**

1 **can (about 8 ounces) tomato sauce**

¼ **teaspoon ground cinnamon**

¼ **teaspoon ground ginger**

1 Coat inside of **CROCK-POT**® slow cooker with nonstick cooking spray. Combine 1 teaspoon chili powder, coriander, ½ teaspoon garlic powder, salt and pepper in small bowl; stir to blend. Brush ribs with 1 tablespoon syrup; rub with spice mixture. Remove ribs to **CROCK-POT**® slow cooker.

2 Combine tomato sauce, remaining 1 teaspoon chili powder, remaining ½ teaspoon garlic powder, remaining 2 tablespoons maple syrup, cinnamon and ginger in medium bowl; stir to blend. Pour tomato sauce mixture over ribs in **CROCK-POT**® slow cooker. Cover; cook on LOW 8 to 9 hours.

3 Remove ribs to large serving platter; cover with foil to keep warm. If desired, remove sauce from **CROCK-POT**® slow cooker to large skillet. Bring to a boil over medium-high heat. Cook 8 to 9 minutes or until sauce is thickened. Brush ribs with sauce and serve any remaining sauce on the side.

Pork Chops with Dried Fruit and Onions

MAKES 6 SERVINGS

6 bone-in end-cut
   pork chops (about
   2½ pounds)

   Salt and black pepper

3 tablespoons vegetable
   oil

2 onions, diced

2 cloves garlic, minced

¼ teaspoon dried sage

¾ cup quartered pitted
   dried plums

¾ cup chopped mixed
   dried fruit

3 cups unsweetened
   unfiltered apple juice

1 whole bay leaf

1 Season pork chops with salt and pepper. Heat oil in large skillet over medium-high heat. Working in batches, brown pork on both sides. Remove to **CROCK-POT**® slow cooker.

2 Add onions to skillet. Reduce heat to medium; cook and stir until softened. Add garlic; cook 30 seconds. Sprinkle sage over mixture. Add dried plums, mixed fruit and apple juice. Bring mixture to a boil. Reduce heat and simmer, uncovered, 3 minutes, stirring to scrape up any browned bits from bottom of skillet. Ladle mixture over pork chops.

3 Add bay leaf. Cover; cook on LOW 3½ to 4 hours or until pork chops are tender. Remove and discard bay leaf. Season with salt and pepper, if desired. Spoon fruit and cooking liquid over pork chops.

CHICKEN AND TURKEY

Lemon and Herb Turkey Breast

MAKES 4 SERVINGS

1 split turkey breast (about 3 pounds)

½ cup lemon juice

½ cup dry white wine

6 cloves garlic, minced

¼ teaspoon salt

¼ teaspoon dried parsley flakes

¼ teaspoon dried tarragon

¼ teaspoon dried rosemary

¼ teaspoon dried sage

¼ teaspoon black pepper

Sprigs fresh sage and rosemary (optional)

Lemon slices (optional)

1 Place turkey in **CROCK-POT**® slow cooker. Combine lemon juice, wine, garlic, salt, parsley flakes, tarragon, rosemary, sage and pepper in medium bowl; stir to blend. Pour lemon juice mixture over turkey in **CROCK-POT**® slow cooker.

2 Cover; cook on LOW 8 to 10 hours or on HIGH 4 to 5 hours. Garnish with fresh sage, fresh rosemary and lemon slices.

Indian-Style Apricot Chicken

MAKES 4 TO 6 SERVINGS

6 **skinless chicken thighs (about 2 pounds)**

¼ **teaspoon salt, plus additional for seasoning**

¼ **teaspoon black pepper, plus additional for seasoning**

1 **tablespoon vegetable oil**

1 **large onion, chopped**

2 **cloves garlic, minced**

2 **tablespoons grated fresh ginger**

½ **teaspoon ground cinnamon**

⅛ **teaspoon ground allspice**

1 **can (about 14 ounces) diced tomatoes**

1 **cup chicken broth**

1 **package (8 ounces) dried apricots**

Pinch saffron threads (optional)

2 **tablespoons chopped fresh Italian parsley (optional)**

1 Coat inside of **CROCK-POT®** slow cooker with nonstick cooking spray. Season chicken with ¼ teaspoon salt and ¼ teaspoon pepper. Heat oil in large skillet over medium-high heat. Brown chicken on all sides. Remove to **CROCK-POT®** slow cooker.

2 Add onion to skillet; cook and stir 3 to 5 minutes or until translucent. Stir in garlic, ginger, cinnamon and allspice; cook and stir 15 to 30 seconds or until mixture is fragrant. Add tomatoes and broth; cook 2 to 3 minutes or until mixture is heated through. Pour into **CROCK-POT®** slow cooker.

3 Add apricots and saffron, if desired. Cover; cook on LOW 5 to 6 hours or on HIGH 3 to 4 hours or until chicken is tender. Season with additional salt and pepper. Garnish with parsley.

Note: To skin chicken easily, grasp skin with paper towel and pull away. Repeat with fresh paper towel for each piece of chicken, discarding skins and towels.

CHICKEN PROVENÇAL

MAKES 8 SERVINGS

2 **pounds boneless, skinless chicken thighs, each cut into quarters**

2 **medium red bell peppers, cut into ¼-inch-thick slices**

1 **medium yellow bell pepper, cut into ¼-inch-thick slices**

1 **onion, thinly sliced**

1 **can (28 ounces) plum tomatoes, drained**

3 **cloves garlic, minced**

¼ **teaspoon salt**

¼ **teaspoon dried thyme**

¼ **teaspoon ground fennel seed**

3 **strips orange peel**

½ **cup fresh basil, chopped**

1 Combine chicken, bell peppers, onion, tomatoes, garlic, salt, thyme, fennel seed and orange peel in **CROCK-POT**® slow cooker; stir to blend.

2 Cover; cook on LOW 7 to 9 hours or on HIGH 4 to 6 hours. Sprinkle with basil just before serving.

Serving Suggestion: This Southern French chicken dish contrasts the citrus with sweetness. Serve with seasonal vegetables.

Note: Recipe can be doubled for a 5-, 6- or 7-quart **CROCK-POT**® slow cooker.

SIMPLE COQ AU VIN

MAKES 4 SERVINGS

4 **chicken legs**

Salt and black pepper

2 **tablespoons olive oil**

8 **ounces mushrooms, sliced**

1 **onion, sliced into rings**

½ **cup dry red wine**

½ **teaspoon dried basil**

½ **teaspoon dried thyme**

½ **teaspoon dried oregano**

1 Season chicken with salt and pepper. Heat oil in large skillet over medium-high heat. Brown chicken on both sides. Remove chicken to **CROCK-POT®** slow cooker.

2 Add mushrooms and onion slices to skillet; cook and stir until onion slices are tender. Add wine, stirring to scrape up any browned bits from bottom of skillet. Add mixture to **CROCK-POT®** slow cooker. Sprinkle with basil, thyme and oregano. Cover; cook on LOW 8 to 10 hours or on HIGH 3 to 4 hours.

3 Serve chicken with sauce.

Turkey Ropa Vieja

MAKES 4 SERVINGS

12 ounces turkey
   tenderloin (2 large
   or 3 small) or
   boneless, skinless
   chicken thighs

1 can (8 ounces) tomato
   sauce

2 medium tomatoes,
   chopped

1 small yellow onion,
   thinly sliced

1 small green bell
   pepper, chopped

4 pimiento-stuffed green
   olives, sliced

1 clove garlic, minced

¾ teaspoon ground
   cumin

½ teaspoon dried
   oregano

⅛ teaspoon black pepper

2 teaspoons lemon juice

¼ teaspoon salt
   (optional)

1 Place turkey in **CROCK-POT**® slow cooker.
Add tomato sauce, tomatoes, onion, bell
pepper, olives, garlic, cumin, oregano and black
pepper. Cover; cook on LOW 6 to 7 hours.

2 Remove turkey to cutting board; shred with
two forks. Return turkey to **CROCK-POT**® slow
cooker. Stir in lemon juice and salt, if desired.

Spicy Turkey with Citrus au Jus

MAKES 6 TO 8 SERVINGS

1 **bone-in turkey breast, thawed, rinsed and patted dry (about 4 pounds)**

¼ **cup (½ stick) butter, softened**

Grated peel of 1 medium lemon

1 **teaspoon chili powder**

¼ **teaspoon black pepper, plus additional for seasoning**

⅛ **to ¼ teaspoon red pepper flakes**

1 **tablespoon lemon juice**

Salt

1 Coat inside of **CROCK-POT®** slow cooker with nonstick cooking spray. Add turkey breast.

2 Mix butter, lemon peel, chili powder, ¼ teaspoon black pepper and red pepper flakes in small bowl until well blended. Spread mixture over top and sides of turkey. Cover; cook on LOW 4 to 5 hours or on HIGH 2½ to 3 hours.

3 Turn off heat. Remove turkey to large cutting board. Cover loosely with foil; let stand 10 to 15 minutes before slicing. Let cooking liquid stand 5 minutes. Skim off and discard fat. Stir lemon juice into cooking liquid. Season with salt and additional black pepper. Serve turkey with sauce.

Curried Chicken and Coconut Soup

MAKES 6 TO 8 SERVINGS

8 large chicken thighs with bones, skin removed

6 cups chicken broth

2 cans (13½ ounces *each*) unsweetened coconut milk

2 bunches green onions, sliced

3 to 4 tablespoons curry powder

4 stalks lemongrass, minced

2 tablespoons peeled and minced fresh ginger

2 packages (6 ounces *each*) baby spinach leaves

3 large limes, divided

Salt and black pepper

1 bunch chopped fresh cilantro

1 Combine chicken, broth, coconut milk, green onions, curry powder, lemongrass and ginger in **CROCK-POT®** slow cooker. Cover; cook on LOW 10 hours or on HIGH 6 hours.

2 Remove chicken to large cutting board. Remove bones; cut chicken into ½-inch cubes. Return chicken to soup; add spinach. Cover; cook on HIGH 10 minutes until spinach is wilted.

3 Juice 2 limes; add juice to **CROCK-POT®** slow cooker. Season soup with salt and pepper. Cut remaining lime into 6 to 8 wedges. Ladle soup into individual serving bowls; sprinkle with cilantro and serve with lime wedges.

Fresh Herbed Turkey Breast

MAKES 8 SERVINGS

2 tablespoons butter, softened

¼ cup fresh sage leaves, minced

¼ cup fresh tarragon, minced

1 clove garlic, minced

1 teaspoon black pepper

½ teaspoon salt

1 split turkey breast (about 4 pounds)

1 Combine butter, sage, tarragon, garlic, pepper and salt in small bowl. Rub butter mixture all over turkey breast.

2 Place turkey breast in **CROCK-POT®** slow cooker. Cover; cook on LOW 8 to 10 hours or on HIGH 4 to 5 hours or until turkey is no longer pink in center.

3 Remove turkey breast to large serving platter. Let stand 10 to 15 minutes. Slice turkey breast. Serve with sauce.

Tip: Fresh herbs enliven this simple, excellent main dish.

Note: Recipe can be doubled for a 5-, 6- or 7-quart **CROCK-POT®** slow cooker.

Forty-Clove Chicken

MAKES 4 TO 6 SERVINGS

1 cut-up whole chicken (about 3 pounds)

Salt and black pepper

1 to 2 tablespoons olive oil

¼ cup dry white wine

2 tablespoons chopped fresh Italian parsley *or* 2 teaspoons dried parsley flakes

2 tablespoons dry vermouth

2 teaspoons dried basil

1 teaspoon dried oregano

Pinch red pepper flakes

40 cloves garlic (about 2 heads)

4 stalks celery, sliced

Juice and peel of 1 lemon

1 Season chicken with salt and black pepper. Heat oil in large skillet over medium heat. Add chicken to skillet; brown on all sides. Remove to platter.

2 Combine wine, parsley, vermouth, basil, oregano and red pepper flakes in large bowl. Add garlic and celery; coat well. Remove garlic and celery to **CROCK-POT**® slow cooker with slotted spoon. Add chicken to remaining herb mixture; coat well. Place chicken on top of garlic mixture in **CROCK-POT**® slow cooker. Sprinkle lemon juice and peel over chicken in **CROCK-POT**® slow cooker. Cover; cook on LOW 6 hours.

BONELESS CHICKEN CACCIATORE

MAKES 6 SERVINGS

1 **tablespoon olive oil**

6 **boneless, skinless chicken breasts, sliced in half horizontally**

4 **cups tomato-basil or marinara pasta sauce**

1 **cup coarsely chopped yellow onion**

1 **cup coarsely chopped green bell pepper**

1 **can (6 ounces) sliced mushrooms**

2 **teaspoons minced garlic**

2 **teaspoons dried oregano**

2 **teaspoons dried thyme**

1 **teaspoon salt**

2 **teaspoons black pepper**

1 Heat oil in large skillet over medium heat. Brown chicken breasts on both sides. Drain and remove to **CROCK-POT®** slow cooker.

2 Add pasta sauce, onion, bell pepper, mushrooms, garlic, oregano, thyme, salt and black pepper to **CROCK-POT®** slow cooker; stir well to combine. Cover; cook on LOW 5 to 7 hours or on HIGH 2 to 3 hours.

BASQUE CHICKEN WITH PEPPERS

MAKES 4 TO 6 SERVINGS

- 1 whole chicken (4 pounds), cut into 8 pieces
- 2 teaspoons salt, divided
- 1 teaspoon black pepper, divided
- 1½ tablespoons olive oil
- 1 onion, chopped
- 1 medium green bell pepper, cut into strips
- 1 medium yellow bell pepper, cut into strips
- 1 medium red bell pepper, cut into strips
- 8 ounces small brown mushrooms, halved
- 1 can (about 14 ounces) stewed tomatoes, undrained
- 1 cup chicken broth
- 3 ounces tomato paste
- 2 cloves garlic, minced
- 1 sprig fresh marjoram
- 1 teaspoon smoked paprika
- 4 ounces chopped prosciutto

1 Season chicken with 1 teaspoon salt and ½ teaspoon black pepper. Heat oil in large skillet over medium-high heat. Add chicken in batches; brown well on all sides. Remove each batch to **CROCK-POT®** slow cooker as it is cooked.

2 Reduce heat to medium-low. Stir in onion; cook and stir 3 minutes or until softened. Add bell peppers and mushrooms; cook 3 minutes. Add tomatoes, broth, tomato paste, garlic, marjoram, remaining 1 teaspoon salt, paprika and remaining ½ teaspoon black pepper to skillet; bring to simmer. Simmer 3 to 4 minutes; pour over chicken.

3 Cover; cook on LOW 5 to 6 hours or on HIGH 4 hours or until chicken is tender. Ladle vegetables and sauce over chicken. Sprinkle with prosciutto.

CHICKEN AND BUTTERNUT SQUASH

MAKES 6 SERVINGS

6 **boneless, skinless chicken thighs (1½ pounds total)**

1 **(1½- to 2-pound) butternut squash, cubed**

2 **tablespoons balsamic vinegar**

4 **cloves garlic, minced**

6 **fresh sage leaves**

Salt and black pepper

Place chicken, squash, vinegar, garlic, sage, salt and pepper in **CROCK-POT®** slow cooker. Cover; cook on LOW 4 to 6 hours.

CHICKEN SOUP

MAKES 4 TO 6 SERVINGS

6 **cups chicken broth**

1½ **pounds boneless, skinless chicken breasts, cubed**

2 **cups sliced carrots**

1 **cup sliced mushrooms**

1 **red bell pepper, chopped**

1 **onion, chopped**

2 **tablespoons grated fresh ginger**

3 **teaspoons minced garlic**

½ **teaspoon red pepper flakes**

Salt and black pepper

Place broth, chicken, carrots, mushrooms, bell pepper, onion, ginger, garlic, red pepper flakes, salt and black pepper in **CROCK-POT®** slow cooker. Cover; cook on LOW 6 to 7 hours or on HIGH 3 to 3½ hours.

Chicken Meatballs in Spicy Tomato Sauce

MAKES 4 SERVINGS

3 tablespoons olive oil, divided

1 medium onion, chopped

6 cloves garlic, minced

1½ teaspoons dried basil

¼ teaspoon red pepper flakes

2 cans (about 14 ounces *each*) diced tomatoes

3 tablespoons tomato paste

2 teaspoons salt, divided

1½ pounds ground chicken

2 egg yolks

1 teaspoon dried oregano

¼ teaspoon black pepper

1 Heat 2 tablespoons oil in large skillet over medium-high heat. Add onion, garlic, basil and red pepper flakes; cook and stir 5 minutes or until onion is softened. Remove half of mixture to **CROCK-POT**® slow cooker. Stir in diced tomatoes, tomato paste and 1 teaspoon salt.

2 Remove remaining onion mixture to large bowl. Add chicken, egg yolks, oregano, remaining 1 teaspoon salt and black pepper; mix well. Form mixture into 24 (1-inch) balls.

3 Heat remaining 1 tablespoon oil in large skillet. Add meatballs in batches; cook 7 minutes or until browned. Remove to **CROCK-POT**® slow cooker using slotted spoon. Cover; cook on LOW 4 to 5 hours.

Chicken Tangier

MAKES 8 SERVINGS

2 tablespoons dried oregano

2 teaspoons seasoned salt

2 teaspoons puréed garlic

¼ teaspoon black pepper

8 skinless chicken thighs (about 3 pounds)

1 lemon, thinly sliced

½ cup dry white wine

2 tablespoons olive oil

1 cup pitted prunes

½ cup pitted green olives

¼ cup currants or raisins

2 tablespoons capers

Chopped fresh Italian parsley or cilantro (optional)

1 Stir oregano, salt, garlic and pepper in small bowl. Rub onto chicken, coating all sides.

2 Coat inside of **CROCK-POT®** slow cooker with nonstick cooking spray. Arrange chicken in **CROCK-POT®** slow cooker, tucking lemon slices between pieces. Pour wine over chicken; sprinkle with oil. Add prunes, olives, currants and capers. Cover; cook on LOW 7 to 8 hours or on HIGH 4 to 5 hours. Garnish with parsley.

Tip: It may seem like a lot, but this recipe really does call for 2 tablespoons dried oregano in order to more accurately represent the powerfully seasoned flavors of Morocco.

OLD WORLD CHICKEN AND VEGETABLES

MAKES 4 SERVINGS

1 **tablespoon dried oregano**

1 **teaspoon salt, divided**

1 **teaspoon paprika**

½ **teaspoon garlic powder**

¼ **teaspoon black pepper**

2 **green bell peppers, cut into thin strips**

1 **yellow onion, thinly sliced**

1 **cut-up whole chicken (about 3 pounds)**

⅓ **cup ketchup**

1 Combine oregano, ½ teaspoon salt, paprika, garlic powder and black pepper in small bowl.

2 Place bell peppers and onion in **CROCK-POT®** slow cooker. Add chicken thighs and legs; sprinkle with half of spice blend. Add chicken breasts; sprinkle with remaining spice blend. Cover; cook on LOW 8 hours or on HIGH 4 hours. Stir in ketchup and remaining ½ teaspoon salt. Serve chicken with vegetables.

CREOLE VEGETABLES AND CHICKEN

MAKES 8 SERVINGS

1 **can (about 14 ounces) diced tomatoes, undrained**

8 **ounces frozen cut okra**

2 **cups chopped green bell pepper**

1 **cup chopped yellow onion**

¾ **cup sliced celery**

1 **cup chicken broth**

2 **teaspoons Worcestershire sauce**

1 **teaspoon dried thyme**

1 **whole bay leaf**

Nonstick cooking spray

1 **pound chicken tenders, cut into bite-size pieces**

¾ **teaspoon Creole seasoning**

1½ **teaspoons sugar**

1 **tablespoon extra virgin olive oil**

Hot pepper sauce

¼ **cup chopped fresh Italian parsley**

1 Coat inside of **CROCK-POT**® slow cooker with cooking spray. Add tomatoes, okra, bell pepper, onion, celery, broth, Worcestershire sauce, thyme and bay leaf. Cover; cook on LOW 9 hours or on HIGH 4½ hours.

2 Coat medium nonstick skillet with cooking spray. Heat over medium-high heat. Add chicken; cook and stir 6 minutes or until beginning to lightly brown. Remove chicken to **CROCK-POT**® slow cooker. Add remaining ingredients except parsley and cook on HIGH 15 minutes to blend flavors. Stir in parsley. Remove and discard bay leaf.

Turkey Chili

MAKES 6 SERVINGS

- **2 tablespoons olive oil, divided**
- **1½ pounds ground turkey**
- **2 medium onions, chopped**
- **1 medium red bell pepper, chopped**
- **1 medium green bell pepper, chopped**
- **5 cloves garlic, minced**
- **1 jalapeño pepper, finely chopped**
- **2 cans (about 14 ounces *each*) fire-roasted diced tomatoes**
- **4 teaspoons chili powder**
- **1 teaspoon ground cumin**
- **1 teaspoon dried oregano**
- **½ teaspoon salt**

1 Heat 1 tablespoon oil in large skillet over medium-high heat. Add turkey; cook 7 to 8 minutes, stirring to break up meat. Remove to **CROCK-POT**® slow cooker.

2 Heat remaining 1 tablespoon oil in same skillet over medium-high heat. Add onions, bell peppers, garlic and jalapeño pepper; cook and stir 4 to 5 minutes or until softened. Stir in tomatoes, chili powder, cumin, oregano and salt; cook 1 minute. Remove onion mixture to **CROCK-POT**® slow cooker. Cover; cook on LOW 6 hours.

Coconut-Curry Chicken Thighs

MAKES 4 SERVINGS

8 **chicken thighs (about 2 to 2½ pounds)**

½ **teaspoon salt**

¼ **teaspoon black pepper**

1 **tablespoon olive oil**

1 **medium onion, chopped**

1 **medium red bell pepper, chopped**

3 **cloves garlic, minced**

1 **tablespoon grated fresh ginger**

1 **can (about 13 ounces) unsweetened coconut milk**

3 **tablespoons honey**

1 **tablespoon Thai red curry paste**

2 **teaspoons Thai roasted red chili paste**

2 **tablespoons chopped fresh cilantro**

½ **cup chopped cashew nuts (optional)**

1 Coat inside of **CROCK-POT®** slow cooker with nonstick cooking spray. Season chicken with salt and pepper. Heat oil in large skillet over medium-high heat. Add chicken; cook 6 to 8 minutes until browned. Remove to **CROCK-POT®** slow cooker.

2 Pour off all but 1 tablespoon of fat from skillet. Heat skillet over medium-high heat. Add onion, bell pepper, garlic and ginger; cook and stir 1 to 2 minutes or until vegetables begin to soften. Remove skillet from heat. Stir in coconut milk, honey, curry paste and chili paste until smooth. Pour coconut mixture over chicken in **CROCK-POT®** slow cooker.

3 Cover; cook on LOW 4 hours. Serve chicken with sauce. Garnish each serving with cilantro and cashews.

Mixed Herb and Butter Rubbed Chicken

MAKES 4 TO 6 SERVINGS

3 **tablespoons butter, softened**

1 **tablespoon grated lemon peel**

2 **teaspoons chopped fresh rosemary**

1 **teaspoon chopped fresh thyme**

¾ **teaspoon salt**

¼ **teaspoon ground black pepper**

1 **whole chicken (4½ to 5 pounds)**

1 Coat inside of **CROCK-POT®** slow cooker with nonstick cooking spray. Combine butter, lemon peel, rosemary, thyme, salt and pepper in small bowl. Loosen skin over breast meat and drumsticks; pat chicken dry with paper towels. Rub butter mixture over and under the chicken skin. Place chicken in **CROCK-POT®** slow cooker.

2 Cover; cook on LOW 5 to 6 hours or until chicken is cooked through, basting every 30 minutes with cooking liquid. Remove chicken to large cutting board. Let stand 15 minutes before carving.

HERBED TURKEY BREAST WITH ORANGE SAUCE

MAKES 4 TO 6 SERVINGS

1 large onion, chopped

3 cloves garlic, minced

1 teaspoon dried rosemary

½ teaspoon black pepper

1 boneless, skinless turkey breast (3 pounds)*

1½ cups orange juice

*Unless you have a 5-, 6- or 7-quart **CROCK-POT®** slow cooker, cut any piece of meat larger than 2½ pounds in half so it cooks completely.

1 Place onion in **CROCK-POT®** slow cooker. Combine garlic, rosemary and pepper in small bowl.

2 Cut slices about three fourths of the way through turkey at 2-inch intervals. Rub garlic mixture between slices. Place turkey, cut side up, in **CROCK-POT®** slow cooker. Pour orange juice over turkey. Cover; cook on LOW 7 to 8 hours.

3 Slice turkey. Serve with orange sauce.

Tip: Don't peek! The **CROCK-POT®** slow cooker can take as long as 30 minutes to regain heat lost when the cover is removed. Only remove the cover when instructed to do so by the recipe.

Curry Chicken with Mango and Red Pepper

MAKES 6 SERVINGS

6 **boneless, skinless chicken thighs or breasts**

Salt and black pepper

2 **tablespoons olive oil**

1 **bag (8 ounces) frozen mango chunks, thawed and drained**

2 **red bell peppers, diced**

⅓ **cup raisins**

1 **shallot, thinly sliced**

¾ **cup chicken broth**

1 **tablespoon cider vinegar**

2 **cloves garlic, crushed**

4 **thin slices fresh ginger**

1 **teaspoon ground cumin**

½ **teaspoon curry powder**

½ **teaspoon whole cloves**

¼ **teaspoon ground red pepper (optional)**

Fresh cilantro (optional)

1 Season chicken with salt and black pepper. Heat oil in large skillet over medium heat. Add chicken; cook 5 to 7 minutes or until lightly browned. Remove to **CROCK-POT**® slow cooker.

2 Add mango, bell peppers, raisins and shallot to **CROCK-POT**® slow cooker. Combine broth, vinegar, garlic, ginger, cumin, curry powder, cloves and ground red pepper, if desired, in large bowl; pour over chicken. Cover; cook on LOW 6 to 8 hours or on HIGH 3 to 4 hours. To serve, spoon mango, raisins and cooking liquid over chicken. Garnish with cilantro.

CHICKEN AND VEGETABLE SOUP

MAKES 10 SERVINGS

1 tablespoon olive oil

2 medium parsnips, cut into ½-inch pieces

2 medium carrots, cut into ½-inch pieces

2 medium onions, chopped

2 stalks celery, cut into ½-inch pieces

1 whole chicken (3 to 3½ pounds)

4 cups chicken broth

10 sprigs fresh Italian parsley *or* 1½ teaspoons dried parsley flakes

4 sprigs fresh thyme *or* ½ teaspoon dried thyme

1 Coat inside of **CROCK-POT®** slow cooker with nonstick cooking spray. Heat oil in large skillet over medium-high heat. Add parsnips, carrots, onions and celery; cook and stir 5 minutes or until vegetables are softened. Remove parsnip mixture to **CROCK-POT®** slow cooker. Add chicken, broth, parsley and thyme.

2 Cover; cook on LOW 6 to 7 hours. Remove chicken to large cutting board; let stand 10 minutes. Remove and discard skin and bones from chicken. Shred chicken using two forks. Stir shredded chicken into **CROCK-POT®** slow cooker.

SATISFYING SEAFOOD

BRAISED SEA BASS WITH AROMATIC VEGETABLES

MAKES 6 SERVINGS

- **2 tablespoons butter or olive oil**
- **2 bulbs fennel, thinly sliced**
- **3 large carrots, julienned**
- **3 large leeks, cleaned and thinly sliced**
- **Kosher salt and black pepper**
- **6 fillets sea bass or other firm-fleshed white fish (2 to 3 pounds total)**

1 Melt butter in large skillet over medium-high heat. Add fennel, carrots and leeks; cook and stir until beginning to soften and lightly brown. Season with salt and pepper. Arrange half of vegetables in bottom of **CROCK-POT®** slow cooker.

2 Season bass with salt and pepper; place on top of vegetables in **CROCK-POT®** slow cooker. Top with remaining vegetables. Cover; cook on LOW 2 to 3 hours or on HIGH 1 to 1½ hours or until fish is cooked through.

COD FISH STEW

MAKES 6 TO 8 SERVINGS

½ **pound bacon, coarsely chopped**

1 **large carrot, diced**

1 **large onion, diced**

2 **stalks celery, diced**

2 **cloves garlic, minced**

Kosher salt and black pepper

3 **cups water**

2 **cups clam juice or fish broth**

1 **can (28 ounces) plum tomatoes, drained**

½ **cup fish broth**

3 **tablespoons chopped fresh Italian parsley**

3 **tablespoons tomato paste**

3 **saffron threads**

2½ **pounds fresh cod, skinned and cut into 1-inch pieces**

1 Heat medium skillet over medium heat. Add bacon; cook and stir until crisp. Add carrot, onion, celery and garlic to skillet; season with salt and pepper. Cook until vegetables soften, stirring frequently.

2 Place bacon and vegetables in **CROCK-POT®** slow cooker. Stir in water, clam juice, tomatoes, broth, parsley, tomato paste and saffron. Cover; cook on LOW 6 to 7 hours or on HIGH 3 to 4 hours.

3 Add cod. Cover; cook on HIGH 10 to 20 minutes or until cod is just cooked through.

Note: Cod is a great fish to use for a soup or stew. The thick, creamy white fish becomes a hearty meal when paired with bacon and tomato.

Mediterranean Shrimp Soup

MAKES 6 SERVINGS

2 **cans (about 14 ounces** *each*) **chicken broth**

1 **can (about 14 ounces) diced tomatoes**

1 **can (8 ounces) tomato sauce**

1 **medium onion, chopped**

½ **medium green bell pepper, chopped**

½ **cup orange juice**

1 **jar (2½ ounces) sliced mushrooms**

¼ **cup sliced pitted black olives**

2 **cloves garlic, minced**

1 **teaspoon dried basil**

2 **whole bay leaves**

¼ **teaspoon whole fennel seed, crushed**

⅛ **teaspoon black pepper**

1 **pound medium raw shrimp, peeled and deveined (with tails on)**

1 Combine broth, tomatoes, tomato sauce, onion, bell pepper, orange juice, mushrooms, olives, garlic, basil, bay leaves, fennel seed and black pepper in **CROCK-POT®** slow cooker; stir to blend. Cover; cook on LOW 4 to 4½ hours or until vegetables are crisp-tender.

2 Stir shrimp into **CROCK-POT®** slow cooker. Cover; cook on LOW 15 to 30 minutes or until shrimp are pink and opaque. Remove and discard bay leaves before serving.

Note: For a heartier soup, add 1 pound firm white fish (such as cod or haddock), cut into 1-inch pieces, 45 minutes before end of cooking time.

Seafood Bouillabaisse

MAKES 4 SERVINGS

Nonstick cooking spray

½ **bulb fennel, chopped**

1 **medium onion, chopped**

2 **cloves garlic, minced**

1 **can (28 ounces) tomato purée**

2 **cans (about 14 ounces each) beef broth**

2 **cups water**

8 **ounces clam juice**

1 **whole bay leaf**

½ **teaspoon salt**

¼ **teaspoon black pepper**

½ **pound red snapper, cut into 1-inch pieces**

8 **mussels, scrubbed and debearded**

8 **cherrystone clams**

8 **large raw shrimp, unpeeled and rinsed (with tails on)**

4 **lemon wedges**

1 Spray large skillet with cooking spray; heat over medium-high heat. Add fennel, onion and garlic; cook and stir 5 minutes or until onion is soft and translucent. Remove fennel mixture to **CROCK-POT**® slow cooker. Add tomato purée, broth, water, clam juice, bay leaf, salt and pepper to **CROCK-POT**® slow cooker. Cover; cook on LOW 6 to 8 hours or on HIGH 3 to 4 hours.

2 Add fish, mussels, clams and shrimp to **CROCK-POT**® slow cooker. Cover; cook on LOW 15 minutes or until fish flakes when tested with fork. Discard any mussels and clams that do not open.

3 Remove and discard bay leaf. Ladle broth into wide soup bowls; top with fish, mussels, clams and shrimp. Squeeze lemon over each serving.

Italian Fish Soup

MAKES 4 SERVINGS

1 **can (about 14 ounces) Italian-seasoned diced tomatoes**

1 **can (about 14 ounces) chicken broth**

1 **small fennel bulb, chopped (about 1 cup), fronds reserved for garnish**

3 **cloves garlic, minced**

1 **tablespoon olive oil**

½ **teaspoon dried basil**

½ **teaspoon crushed saffron threads (optional)**

¼ **teaspoon red pepper flakes**

½ **pound (8 ounces) skinless halibut or cod fillets, cut into 1-inch pieces**

½ **pound (8 ounces) raw medium shrimp, peeled and deveined (with tails on)**

1 Combine tomatoes, broth, fennel bulb, garlic, oil, basil, saffron, if desired, and red pepper flakes in **CROCK-POT**® slow cooker. Cover; cook on LOW 4 to 5 hours or on HIGH 2½ to 3 hours or until fennel is tender.

2 Stir in halibut and shrimp. Cover; cook on HIGH 15 to 30 minutes or until shrimp are pink and opaque and fish begins to flake when tested with fork. Ladle soup evenly into shallow bowls. Garnish with chopped fennel fronds.

BACON-WRAPPED SCALLOPS

MAKES 12 SERVINGS

24 **sea scallops, side muscle removed**

½ **cup fish broth**

3 **tablespoons chopped fresh cilantro**

2 **tablespoons honey**

¼ **teaspoon ground chipotle chili powder**

12 **slices bacon, halved**

1 Pour ½-inch of water in bottom of **CROCK-POT®** slow cooker. Combine scallops, broth, cilantro, honey and chipotle chili powder in medium bowl; stir to coat. Refrigerate 30 minutes.

2 Place 1 scallop on 1 bacon half. Roll up jelly-roll style and secure with toothpick. Remove to large skillet. Repeat with remaining bacon and scallops.

3 Heat skillet over medium heat. Cook scallops 3 to 5 minutes or until bacon is just beginning to brown. Remove to **CROCK-POT®** slow cooker.

4 Cover; cook on LOW 1 hour. Serve warm or at room temperature.

Cape Cod Stew

MAKES 8 SERVINGS

2 **pounds medium raw shrimp, peeled and deveined**

2 **pounds fresh cod or other white fish**

3 **lobsters (1½ to 2½ pounds *each*), uncooked**

1 **pound mussels or clams, scrubbed**

2 **cans (about 14 ounces *each*) chopped tomatoes**

4 **cups beef broth**

½ **cup chopped onions**

½ **cup chopped carrots**

½ **cup chopped fresh cilantro**

2 **tablespoons sea salt**

2 **teaspoons crushed or minced garlic**

2 **teaspoons lemon juice**

4 **whole bay leaves**

1 **teaspoon dried thyme**

½ **teaspoon saffron threads**

1 Cut shrimp and fish into bite-size pieces and place in large bowl; refrigerate. Remove lobster tails and claws. Chop tail into 2-inch pieces and separate claws at joints. Place lobster and mussels in large bowl; refrigerate.

2 Combine remaining ingredients in **CROCK-POT®** slow cooker. Cover; cook on LOW 7 hours.

3 Add seafood. Turn **CROCK-POT®** slow cooker to HIGH. Cover; cook on HIGH 45 minutes to 1 hour or until seafood is just cooked through. Remove and discard bay leaves. Discard any mussels that do not open.

Cioppino

MAKES 6 SERVINGS

1 pound cod, halibut or any firm-fleshed white fish, cubed

1 cup sliced mushrooms

2 carrots, sliced

1 onion, chopped

1 green bell pepper, chopped

1 teaspoon minced garlic

1 can (15 ounces) tomato sauce

1 can (about 14 ounces) beef broth

1 teaspoon salt

½ teaspoon black pepper

½ teaspoon dried oregano

1 can (7 ounces) cooked clams

½ pound cooked shrimp

1 package (6 ounces) cooked crabmeat

Minced fresh Italian parsley

1 Combine cod, mushrooms, carrots, onion, bell pepper, garlic, tomato sauce, broth, salt, black pepper and oregano in **CROCK-POT®** slow cooker. Cover; cook on LOW 10 to 12 hours.

2 Turn **CROCK-POT®** slow cooker to HIGH. Add clams, shrimp and crabmeat. Cover; cook on HIGH 30 minutes or until seafood is heated through. Garnish with parsley.

SLOW COOKER SALMON WITH BEER

MAKES 4 SERVINGS

4 **salmon fillets (6 ounces *each*)**

Salt and black pepper

1 **cup Italian dressing**

3 **tablespoons olive oil**

1 **yellow bell pepper, sliced**

1 **red bell pepper, sliced**

1 **orange bell pepper, sliced**

1 **large onion, sliced**

2 **cloves garlic, minced**

1 **teaspoon lemon peel**

½ **teaspoon dried basil**

2 **cups spinach, stems removed**

¾ **cup fish broth**

½ **lemon, cut into quarters**

1 Season both sides of fillets with salt and black pepper. Place fillets in baking dish; pour Italian dressing over fillets. Cover and refrigerate 30 minutes or up to 2 hours. Discard marinade.

2 Pour oil into **CROCK-POT**® slow cooker; lay salmon fillets on top of oil, stacking as necessary. Top with bell peppers, onion, garlic, lemon peel and basil. Cover with spinach. Pour broth over all in **CROCK-POT**® slow cooker.

3 Cover; cook on HIGH 1½ hours. Remove fillets to platter; top with vegetables. Squeeze lemon over salmon.

PALEO SHRIMP AND OKRA GUMBO

MAKES 6 SERVINGS

1 **tablespoon olive oil**

8 **ounces kielbasa, halved lengthwise and cut into ¼-inch-thick half moons**

1 **green bell pepper, chopped**

1 **medium onion, chopped**

3 **stalks celery, cut into ¼-inch slices**

6 **green onions, chopped**

4 **cloves garlic, minced**

1 **cup chicken broth**

1 **can (about 14 ounces) diced tomatoes**

1 **teaspoon Cajun seasoning**

½ **teaspoon dried thyme**

1 **pound large shrimp, peeled and deveined (with tails on)**

2 **cups frozen cut okra, thawed**

1 Coat inside of **CROCK-POT**® slow cooker with nonstick cooking spray. Heat oil in large skillet over medium-high heat. Add kielbasa; cook and stir 4 minutes until browned. Remove to **CROCK-POT**® slow cooker.

2 Return skillet to medium-high heat. Add bell pepper, chopped onion, celery, green onions and garlic; cook and stir 5 to 6 minutes until vegetables are crisp-tender. Remove to **CROCK-POT**® slow cooker. Stir in broth, tomatoes, Cajun seasoning and thyme.

3 Cover; cook on LOW 4 hours. Stir in shrimp and okra. Cover; cook on LOW 1 hour.

Seafood Cioppino

MAKES 4 SERVINGS

1 **tablespoon olive oil**

1 **medium fennel bulb, thinly sliced**

1 **medium onion, chopped**

4 **cloves garlic, minced**

1 **teaspoon dried basil**

¼ **teaspoon saffron threads, crushed (optional)**

1 **can (about 14 ounces) diced tomatoes**

1 **bottle (8 ounces) clam juice**

16 **little neck clams, scrubbed**

24 **mussels, scrubbed**

1 **pound cod fillet, cut into 8 pieces**

8 **ounces large shrimp, peeled and deveined (with tails on)**

½ **teaspoon salt**

⅛ **teaspoon black pepper**

1 Coat inside of **CROCK-POT®** slow cooker with nonstick cooking spray. Heat oil in large skillet over medium-high heat. Add fennel, onion, garlic, basil and saffron, if desired; cook and stir 4 to 5 minutes or until vegetables are softened. Remove onion mixture to **CROCK-POT®** slow cooker. Stir in tomatoes and clam juice.

2 Cover; cook on HIGH 2 to 3 hours. Add clams. Cover; cook on HIGH 30 minutes. Add mussels. Cover; cook on HIGH 15 minutes.

3 Season cod and shrimp with salt and pepper. Place on top of shellfish. Cover; cook on HIGH 25 to 30 minutes until clams and mussels have opened and fish is cooked through.

Scallops in Fresh Tomato and Herb Sauce

MAKES 4 SERVINGS

2 **tablespoons vegetable oil**

1 **medium red onion, peeled and diced**

1 **clove garlic, minced**

3½ **cups fresh tomatoes, peeled***

1 **can (12 ounces) tomato pureé**

1 **can (6 ounces) tomato paste**

¼ **cup fish broth**

2 **tablespoons chopped fresh Italian parsley**

1 **tablespoon chopped fresh oregano**

¼ **teaspoon black pepper**

1½ **pounds fresh scallops, cleaned and drained**

*To peel tomatoes, place one at a time in simmering water about 10 seconds. (Add 30 seconds if tomatoes are not fully ripened.) Immediately plunge into a bowl of cold water for another 10 seconds. Peel skin with a knife.

1 Heat oil in medium skillet over medium heat. Add onion and garlic; cook and stir 7 to 8 minutes or until onion is soft and translucent. Remove to **CROCK-POT**® slow cooker.

2 Add tomatoes, tomato purée, tomato paste, broth, parsley, oregano and pepper. Cover; cook on LOW 6 to 8 hours.

3 Turn **CROCK-POT**® slow cooker to HIGH. Add scallops. Cover; cook on HIGH 15 minutes or until scallops are cooked through.

Lemon and Garlic Shrimp

MAKES 6 TO 8 SERVINGS

1 **pound large raw shrimp, peeled and deveined (with tails on)**

½ **cup (1 stick) unsalted butter, cubed**

3 **cloves garlic, crushed**

2 **tablespoons lemon juice**

½ **teaspoon paprika**

   Salt and black pepper

2 **tablespoons finely chopped fresh Italian parsley**

1 Coat inside of **CROCK-POT®** slow cooker with nonstick cooking spray. Add shrimp, butter and garlic; mix well. Cover; cook on HIGH 1¼ hours.

2 Turn off heat. Stir in lemon juice, paprika, salt and pepper. Spoon shrimp and liquid into large serving bowl. Sprinkle with parsley.

Cod Tapenade

MAKES 4 SERVINGS

4 **cod fillets or other firm white fish (2 to 3 pounds total)**

   Salt and black pepper

2 **lemons, thinly sliced**

   Tapenade (recipe follows)

1 Season cod with salt and pepper.

2 Arrange half of lemon slices in bottom of **CROCK-POT®** slow cooker. Top with cod; cover with remaining lemon slices. Cover; cook on HIGH 1 hour or until fish is just cooked through (actual time depends on thickness of fish).

3 Remove fish to serving plates; discard lemon. Prepare and top with Tapenade.

Tapenade

MAKES ABOUT 1 CUP

½ **pound pitted kalamata olives**

2 **tablespoons chopped fresh thyme or Italian parsley**

2 **tablespoons capers, drained**

2 **tablespoons anchovy paste**

1 **clove garlic**

¼ **teaspoon grated orange peel**

⅛ **teaspoon ground red pepper**

½ **cup olive oil**

Place olives, thyme, capers, anchovy paste, garlic, orange peel and ground red pepper in food processor or blender; pulse to roughly chop. Add oil; pulse briefly to form a chunky paste.

Zuppa de Clams

MAKES 3 TO 4 SERVINGS

1   **package (8 ounces) shiitake mushrooms**

1   **red onion, diced**

½   **pound cooked chorizo sausage, thinly sliced**

1½ **cups homemade or best quality tomato sauce**

1½ **cups fish broth**

24 **littleneck clams, scrubbed and rinsed**

1 Heat large skillet over medium heat. Add mushrooms, onion and sausage; cook 8 minutes or until onion softens, stirring frequently. Remove to **CROCK-POT®** slow cooker.

2 Add tomato sauce and broth to **CROCK-POT®** slow cooker. Cover; cook on LOW 6 to 7 hours or on HIGH 3½ hours. Add clams; cover and cook on HIGH 10 to 15 minutes or until clams open. Discard any clams that do not open; serve.

FRUITS AND VEGETABLES

Spiced Vanilla Applesauce

MAKES 6 CUPS

5 pounds (about 10 medium) sweet apples (such as Fuji or Gala), peeled and cut into 1-inch pieces

½ cup water

2 teaspoons vanilla

1 teaspoon ground cinnamon

¼ teaspoon ground nutmeg

¼ teaspoon ground cloves

1 Combine apples, water, vanilla, cinnamon, nutmeg and cloves in **CROCK-POT**® slow cooker; stir to blend. Cover; cook on HIGH 3 to 4 hours or until apples are very tender.

2 Turn off heat. Mash mixture with potato masher to smooth out any large lumps. Let cool completely before serving.

LEMON CAULIFLOWER

MAKES 6 SERVINGS

1 tablespoon butter

3 cloves garlic, minced

2 tablespoons lemon juice

½ cup water

4 tablespoons chopped fresh Italian parsley, divided

½ teaspoon grated lemon peel

6 cups (about 1½ pounds) cauliflower florets

¼ cup grated Parmesan cheese

Lemon slices (optional)

1 Heat butter in small saucepan over medium heat. Add garlic; cook and stir 2 to 3 minutes or until soft. Stir in lemon juice and water.

2 Combine garlic mixture, 1 tablespoon parsley, lemon peel and cauliflower in **CROCK-POT**® slow cooker; stir to blend. Cover; cook on LOW 4 hours.

3 Sprinkle with remaining 3 tablespoons parsley and cheese before serving. Garnish with lemon slices.

Creamy Sweet Potato and Butternut Squash Soup

MAKES 4 TO 6 SERVINGS

1 **pound butternut squash, diced into 1-inch cubes (about 3½ cups total)**

1 **pound sweet potatoes, cut into 1-inch cubes (about 3 cups total)**

½ **cup chopped onion**

1 **can (about 14 ounces) vegetable broth, divided**

½ **cup (1 stick) butter, cubed**

1 **can (about 13 ounces) unsweetened coconut milk**

1½ **teaspoons salt**

½ **teaspoon ground cumin**

½ **teaspoon ground red pepper**

3 **to 4 green onions, finely chopped (optional)**

1 Combine squash, sweet potatoes, onion, half of broth and butter in **CROCK-POT®** slow cooker. Cover; cook on HIGH 4 hours or until vegetables are tender.

2 Process mixture in blender, 1 cup at a time, until smooth, returning batches to **CROCK-POT®** slow cooker as they are processed. Stir in remaining broth, coconut milk, salt, cumin and ground red pepper. Cover; cook on HIGH until heated through. To serve, ladle into bowls; sprinkle with chopped green onions, if desired.

GINGER PEAR CIDER

MAKES 8 TO 10 SERVINGS

8 **cups pear juice or cider**

¾ **cup lemon juice**

¼ **to ½ cup honey**

10 **whole cloves**

2 **cinnamon sticks**

8 **slices fresh ginger**

1 Combine pear juice, lemon juice, honey, cloves, cinnamon sticks and ginger in 3½- to 4-quart **CROCK-POT**® slow cooker. Cover; cook on LOW 5 to 6 hours or on HIGH 2½ to 3 hours.

2 Remove and discard cloves, cinnamon sticks and ginger before serving. Turn **CROCK-POT**® slow cooker to WARM setting to serve.

Collard Greens

MAKES 10 SERVINGS

4 **bunches collard greens, stemmed, washed and torn into bite-size pieces**

2 **cups water**

½ **medium red bell pepper, cut into strips**

⅓ **medium green bell pepper, cut into strips**

¼ **cup olive oil**

¼ **teaspoon salt**

¼ **teaspoon black pepper**

Combine collard greens, water, bell peppers, oil, salt and black pepper in **CROCK-POT®** slow cooker. Cover; cook on LOW 3 to 4 hours or on HIGH 2 hours or until heated through.

Eggplant Italiano

MAKES 6 SERVINGS

1¼ **pounds eggplant, cut into 1-inch cubes**

2 **onions, thinly sliced**

2 **stalks celery, cut into 1-inch pieces**

1 **can (about 14 ounces) diced tomatoes**

3 **tablespoons tomato sauce**

1 **tablespoon olive oil**

½ **cup sliced black olives**

2 **tablespoons balsamic vinegar**

1 **tablespoon sugar**

1 **tablespoon capers, drained**

1 **teaspoon dried oregano or basil**

Salt and black pepper

1 Combine eggplant, onions, celery, tomatoes, tomato sauce and oil in **CROCK-POT**® slow cooker. Cover; cook on LOW 3½ to 4 hours or until eggplant is tender.

2 Stir olives, vinegar, sugar, capers and oregano into **CROCK-POT**® slow cooker. Season with salt and pepper. Cover; cook on LOW 45 minutes or until heated through.

OLIVE OIL MASHED RUTABAGAS

MAKES 8 SERVINGS

1 (2½ to 3-pound)
   rutabaga (waxed
   turnip), peeled and
   cut into 1-inch pieces

4 cloves garlic

   Boiling water

2 tablespoons olive oil

1 teaspoon salt

1 teaspoon dried thyme

1 Combine rutabaga, garlic and enough boiling water to cover by 1 inch in **CROCK-POT®** slow cooker. Cover; cook on LOW 7 to 8 hours.

2 Place rutabaga in food processor or blender; purée, adding boiling water as necessary to reach desired consistency. Stir in oil, salt and thyme.

Mushroom Soup

MAKES 4 TO 6 SERVINGS

2 tablespoons olive oil

2 large Vidalia onions, coarsely chopped

1 package (10 ounces) cremini mushrooms

1 package (10 ounces) button mushrooms

Salt and black pepper

2 tablespoons butter

6 to 10 cloves garlic, peeled and coarsely chopped

4 cups plus 2 tablespoons beef broth, divided

1 Heat oil in large skillet over medium-high heat. Add onions, mushrooms, salt and pepper; cook and stir 8 to 10 minutes or until softened.

2 Add butter and garlic; cook 1 to 2 minutes. Add 2 tablespoons broth, scraping up any brown bits from bottom of skillet. Add vegetable mixture and remaining 4 cups broth to **CROCK-POT**® slow cooker. Cover; cook on LOW 5 to 6 hours or on HIGH 3 to 4 hours.

Note: Mushroom soup is usually made with beef broth, because the deep flavor of the mushrooms balances perfectly with a hearty broth. Try experimenting with a variety of mushrooms, but don't use wild mushrooms only. Although they add great flavor, they can be too intense if used exclusively.

Slow Cooker Veggie Stew

MAKES 4 TO 6 SERVINGS

1 tablespoon vegetable oil

⅔ cup carrot slices

½ cup diced onion

2 cloves garlic, chopped

2 cans (about 14 ounces *each*) vegetable broth

1½ cups chopped green cabbage

½ cup cut green beans

½ cup diced zucchini

1 tablespoon tomato paste

½ teaspoon dried basil

½ teaspoon dried oregano

¼ teaspoon salt

1 Heat oil in medium skillet over medium-high heat. Add carrot, onion and garlic; cook and stir until tender.

2 Remove carrot mixture to **CROCK-POT**® slow cooker. Stir in remaining ingredients. Cover; cook on LOW 8 to 10 hours or on HIGH 4 to 5 hours.

Curried Butternut Squash Soup

MAKES 6 TO 8 SERVINGS

2 pounds butternut squash, rinsed, peeled, cored and chopped into 1-inch cubes

1 firm crisp apple, peeled, cored and chopped

1 yellow onion, chopped

5 cups chicken broth

1 tablespoon curry powder, sweet or hot

¼ teaspoon ground cloves

Salt and black pepper

¼ cup chopped dried cranberries (optional)

1 Place squash, apple and onion in **CROCK-POT®** slow cooker.

2 Combine broth, curry powder and cloves in small bowl. Pour mixture into **CROCK-POT®** slow cooker. Cover; cook on LOW 5 to 5½ hours or on HIGH 4 hours or until vegetables are tender.

3 Process soup in blender, in 2 or 3 batches, to desired consistency. Season with salt and pepper. Garnish with cranberries.

Caramelized Onion Sauce

MAKES ABOUT 3 CUPS

½ **cup (1 stick) butter, cut into pieces**

3 **pounds onions**

2 **teaspoons balsamic vinegar**

1 **teaspoon salt**

½ **teaspoon black pepper**

½ **cup beef broth**

1 Coat inside of **CROCK-POT**® slow cooker with nonstick cooking spray. Place butter in **CROCK-POT**® slow cooker. Cover; cook on HIGH until melted.

2 Meanwhile, slice onions in half through stem ends. Remove outer peels and place flat on cutting bpard. Slice onions thinly, holding knife at an angle, cutting through to center. Add to melted butter in **CROCK-POT**® slow cooker. Stir in vinegar, salt and pepper. Turn **CROCK-POT**® slow cooker to LOW. Cook, uncovered, on LOW 8 to 10 hours or until onions are brown, soft and reduced in volume to about 3 cups.

3 Stir in broth, stirring to scrape up browned bits. Serve immediately or cool to room temperature and refrigerate in airtight container until needed. Reheat before serving.

Serving Suggestion: This onion sauce is fabulous served over your favorite roasted poultry or meat.

TIP: For a thicker sauce, add broth and turn **CROCK-POT**® slow cooker to HIGH. Cook, uncovered, on HIGH until desired consistency.

Winter Squash and Apples

MAKES 4 TO 6 SERVINGS

1 **teaspoon salt, plus additional for seasoning**

½ **teaspoon black pepper, plus additional for seasoning**

1 **butternut squash (about 2 pounds)**

2 **apples, sliced**

1 **medium onion, quartered and sliced**

1½ **tablespoons butter**

1 Combine 1 teaspoon salt and ½ teaspoon pepper in small bowl.

2 Cut squash into 2-inch pieces; place in **CROCK-POT**® slow cooker. Add apples and onion. Sprinkle with salt and pepper mixture; stir well. Cover; cook on LOW 6 to 7 hours or until vegetables are tender.

3 Stir in butter and season to taste with additional salt and pepper.

Spiced Apple Tea

MAKES 4 SERVINGS

3 **bags cinnamon herbal tea**

3 **cups boiling water**

2 **cups unsweetened apple juice**

6 **whole cloves**

1 **cinnamon stick**

1 Place tea bags in **CROCK-POT®** slow cooker. Pour boiling water over tea bags; cover and let stand 10 minutes. Remove and discard tea bags.

2 Add apple juice, cloves and cinnamon stick to **CROCK-POT®** slow cooker. Cover; cook on LOW 2 to 3 hours. Remove and discard cloves and cinnamon stick. Serve warm in mugs.

Mexican-Style Spinach

MAKES 6 SERVINGS

3 **packages (10 ounces *each*) frozen chopped spinach**

1 **tablespoon canola oil**

1 **onion, chopped**

1 **clove garlic, minced**

2 **Anaheim chiles, roasted, peeled and minced***

3 **fresh tomatillos, roasted, husks removed and chopped****

*To roast chiles, heat large heavy skillet over medium-high heat. Add chiles; cook and turn until blackened all over. Place chiles in brown paper bag 2 to 5 minutes. Remove chiles from bag; scrape off charred skin. Cut off top and pull out core. Slice lengthwise; scrape off veins and any remaining seeds with a knife.

**To roast tomatillos, heat large heavy skillet over medium heat. Add tomatillos with papery husks; cook 10 minutes or until husks are brown and interior flesh is soft. Remove and discard husks when cool enough to handle.

Place spinach in **CROCK-POT**® slow cooker. Heat oil in large skillet over medium heat. Add onion and garlic; cook and stir 5 minutes or until onion is tender. Add chiles and tomatillos; cook 3 to 4 minutes. Remove onion mixture to **CROCK-POT**® slow cooker. Cover; cook on LOW 4 to 6 hours.

Simmered Napa Cabbage with Dried Apricots

MAKES 4 SERVINGS

4 cups napa cabbage
    or green cabbage,
    cored, cleaned and
    sliced thin

1 cup chopped dried
    apricots

¼ cup clover honey

2 tablespoons orange
    juice

½ cup vegetable broth

   Salt and black pepper

   Grated orange peel
   (optional)

1 Combine cabbage and apricots in **CROCK-POT®** slow cooker; toss well.

2 Combine honey and orange juice in small bowl; stir until smooth. Drizzle over cabbage. Add broth. Cover; cook on LOW 5 to 6 hours or on HIGH 2 to 3 hours or until cabbage is tender.

3 Season with salt and pepper. Garnish with orange peel.

Curried Sweet Potato and Carrot Soup

MAKES 8 SERVINGS

- 4 **cups vegetable broth**
- 2 **medium to large sweet potatoes, cut into ¾-inch dice (about 5 cups)**
- 2 **cups baby carrots**
- 1 **small onion, chopped**
- ¾ **teaspoon curry powder**
- ½ **teaspoon salt**
- ½ **teaspoon black pepper**
- ½ **teaspoon ground cinnamon**
- ¼ **teaspoon ground ginger**
- ¾ **cup half-and-half**
- 1 **tablespoon maple syrup**
- **Candied ginger (optional)**

1 Combine broth, sweet potatoes, carrots, onion, curry powder, salt, pepper, cinnamon and ground ginger in **CROCK-POT®** slow cooker; stir to blend. Cover; cook on LOW 7 to 8 hours.

2 Pour soup, 1 cup at a time, into food processor or blender; process until smooth. Return soup to **CROCK-POT®** slow cooker after each batch. Add half-and-half and maple syrup; stir to blend. Turn **CROCK-POT®** slow cooker to HIGH. Cover; cook on HIGH 15 minutes or until heated through. Garnish each serving with candied ginger.

MULLED CRAN-APPLE PUNCH

MAKES 8 SERVINGS

1 **orange**

1 **lemon**

1 **lime**

15 **whole black peppercorns**

10 **whole cloves**

10 **whole allspice**

3 **cinnamon sticks**

6 **cups apple juice**

3 **cups cranberry juice**

3 **tablespoons maple syrup**

1 Use vegetable peeler to remove 5 to 6 (2- to 3-inch-long) sections of orange, lemon and lime peel, being careful to avoid white pith. Squeeze juice from orange, reserve. Cut 5-inch double-thickness cheesecloth square. Place peels, peppercorns, cloves, allspice and cinnamon sticks in center of cheesecloth; bring corners together; tie with cotton string or strip of additional cheesecloth.

2 Pour apple juice, cranberry juice, maple syrup and reserved orange juice into 3½- to 4-quart **CROCK-POT**® slow cooker; add spice bag. Cover; cook on LOW 5 to 6 hours or on HIGH 2½ to 3 hours. Turn **CROCK-POT**® slow cooker to WARM setting to serve.

Autumn Apple and Squash Soup

MAKES 6 TO 8 SERVINGS

5 **tablespoons butter**

2½ **pounds butternut squash, peeled, seeded and cut into ½-inch pieces (about 6 cups)**

2 **large red onions**

3 **to 4 large stalks celery**

3 **large green apples, peeled, cored and coarsely chopped**

2 **to 3 fresh thyme sprigs, stemmed**

10 **fresh sage leaves, minced**

4 **cups vegetable broth**

Kosher salt and black pepper

½ **cup pepitas***

1 **tablespoon honey**

1 **tablespoon water**

Extra virgin olive oil (optional)

*Pepitas, or shelled pumpkin seeds, are available at specialty and Latin food stores and make a great garnish to almost any soup or salad. They can be seasoned as desired and lightly toasted in a skillet on the stovetop.

1 Melt butter in large heavy saucepan over medium-high heat. Add squash, onions and celery; cook and stir 15 minutes or until slightly softened. Place vegetables in **CROCK-POT®** slow cooker. Mix in apples, thyme and sage. Add broth; cook on LOW 12 hours or on HIGH 8 hours.

2 Working in batches, purée soup in blender, pulsing to achieve coarser or smoother texture as desired. Return soup to **CROCK-POT®** slow cooker; set to WARM. (If soup has cooled considerably, set to HIGH.) Taste and adjust seasonings.

3 Combine pepitas with honey and water in small skillet over medium heat. Toast lightly. Ladle soup into bowls. Top with honeyed pepitas. Drizzle with olive oil.

Variations: Add lump crabmeat during last 15 minutes of cooking.

Brussels Sprouts with Bacon, Thyme and Raisins

MAKES 8 SERVINGS

2 pounds Brussels sprouts

1 cup vegetable broth

⅔ cup golden raisins

2 thick slices applewood smoked bacon, chopped

2 tablespoons chopped fresh thyme

Trim ends from sprouts; cut in half lengthwise through core (or in quarters). Combine sprouts, broth, raisins, bacon and thyme in **CROCK-POT®** slow cooker; stir to blend. Cover; cook on LOW 3 to 4 hours.

Fennel Braised with Tomato

MAKES 6 SERVINGS

2 **bulbs fennel**

1 **tablespoon olive oil**

1 **onion, sliced**

1 **clove garlic, sliced**

4 **tomatoes, chopped**

⅔ **cup plus 3 tablespoons vegetable broth**

1 **tablespoon chopped fresh marjoram *or* 1 teaspoon dried marjoram**

Salt and black pepper

1 Trim stems and bottoms from fennel bulbs, reserving green leafy tops for garnish. Cut each bulb lengthwise into four wedges.

2 Heat oil in large skillet over medium heat. Add fennel, onion and garlic; cook and stir 5 minutes or until onion is soft and translucent. Remove fennel mixture to **CROCK-POT**® slow cooker. Add tomatoes, broth, marjoram, salt and pepper; stir to blend.

3 Cover; cook on LOW 2 to 3 hours or on HIGH 1 to 1½ hours. Garnish with reserved green leafy tops.

Bagna Cauda

MAKES 1⅓ CUPS

¾ **cup olive oil**

6 **tablespoons butter, softened**

12 **anchovy fillets, drained**

6 **cloves garlic**

⅛ **teaspoon red pepper flakes**

Optional dippers: sugar snap peas, bell pepper slices, green onions, cucumber spears, zucchini spears and/or carrot sticks

1 Place oil, butter, anchovies, garlic and red pepper flakes in food processor or blender; process 30 seconds or until smooth. Heat medium saucepan over medium heat. Pour oil mixture into saucepan; bring to a boil. Reduce heat to medium low; simmer 5 minutes.

2 Coat inside of **CROCK-POT® LITTLE DIPPER®** slow cooker with nonstick cooking spray. Fill with warm dip. Serve with desired dippers.

VOLUME MEASUREMENTS (dry)

$^1/_8$ teaspoon = 0.5 mL
$^1/_4$ teaspoon = 1 mL
$^1/_2$ teaspoon = 2 mL
$^3/_4$ teaspoon = 4 mL
1 teaspoon = 5 mL
1 tablespoon = 15 mL
2 tablespoons = 30 mL
$^1/_4$ cup = 60 mL
$^1/_3$ cup = 75 mL
$^1/_2$ cup = 125 mL
$^2/_3$ cup = 150 mL
$^3/_4$ cup = 175 mL
1 cup = 250 mL
2 cups = 1 pint = 500 mL
3 cups = 750 mL
4 cups = 1 quart = 1 L

VOLUME MEASUREMENTS (fluid)

1 fluid ounce (2 tablespoons) = 30 mL
4 fluid ounces ($^1/_2$ cup) = 125 mL
8 fluid ounces (1 cup) = 250 mL
12 fluid ounces (1$^1/_2$ cups) = 375 mL
16 fluid ounces (2 cups) = 500 mL

WEIGHTS (mass)

$^1/_2$ ounce = 15 g
1 ounce = 30 g
3 ounces = 90 g
4 ounces = 120 g
8 ounces = 225 g
10 ounces = 285 g
12 ounces = 360 g
16 ounces = 1 pound = 450 g

DIMENSIONS

$^1/_{16}$ inch = 2 mm
$^1/_8$ inch = 3 mm
$^1/_4$ inch = 6 mm
$^1/_2$ inch = 1.5 cm
$^3/_4$ inch = 2 cm
1 inch = 2.5 cm

OVEN TEMPERATURES

250°F = 120°C
275°F = 140°C
300°F = 150°C
325°F = 160°C
350°F = 180°C
375°F = 190°C
400°F = 200°C
425°F = 220°C
450°F = 230°C

BAKING PAN SIZES

Utensil	Size in Inches/Quarts	Metric Volume	Size in Centimeters
Baking or Cake Pan (square or rectangular)	8×8×2	2 L	20×20×5
	9×9×2	2.5 L	23×23×5
	12×8×2	3 L	30×20×5
	13×9×2	3.5 L	33×23×5
Loaf Pan	8×4×3	1.5 L	20×10×7
	9×5×3	2 L	23×13×7
Round Layer Cake Pan	8×1½	1.2 L	20×4
	9×1½	1.5 L	23×4
Pie Plate	8×1¼	750 mL	20×3
	9×1¼	1 L	23×3
Baking Dish or Casserole	1 quart	1 L	—
	1½ quart	1.5 L	—
	2 quart	2 L	—